CONTEMPORARY PAINTERS

JAMES THRALL SOBY

CONTEMPORARY

Painters

THE MUSEUM OF MODERN ART

NEW YORK

REPRINT EDITION, 1966   PUBLISHED FOR
THE MUSEUM OF MODERN ART BY ARNO PRESS

FOR ALFRED BARR AND DOROTHY MILLER,
WHOM I DEEPLY REVERE

CONTENTS

ACKNOWLEDGMENT

By permission of the publishers, several of the following chapters have appeared as magazine articles: "Italy: Two Movements and Two Paintings" in the *Magazine of Art* for February, 1946; "Matta Echaurren" in the same magazine, March, 1947; "Ben Shahn and Morris Graves" in the American number of *Horizon,* October, 1947. Much of the material in "Younger American Painters" was used in an article for *Harper's Bazaar,* September, 1947.

I am most of all indebted to Mr. Alfred H. Barr, Jr., to whom all of us working in the contemporary field owe an immeasurable debt, and whose editorial guidance has been generous and valuable. Miss Dorothy C. Miller has made many welcome suggestions as to the contents of the chapters on American painters. Mr. Curt Valentin has performed a similar service for the chapter on Max Beckmann. Mrs. Mimi Catlin and Miss Pearl Moeller of the Museum of Modern Art staff have helped greatly in locating many of the photographs reproduced. And last but by no means least, I wish to thank my wife, Eleanor Howland Soby, for her work and encouragement.

J.T.S.

PREFACE

In selecting the painters and movements hereinafter discussed, I have had in mind, except in the opening two chapters, the amount of recent critical material available in English. There is already, I believe, too much duplication of subject in books on modern art. I have striven to avoid it here, sometimes by re-exploring neglected movements like vorticism and the scuola metafisica, *sometimes by proposing what I hope are tenable if untried juxtapositions and categories, again by writing about young or lesser known artists—the newer American and English painters, for example. I have included several artists whose fame has outgrown the critical texts in English on their works, notably Max Beckmann.*

I have also tried, though less deliberately, to suggest modern painting's astonishing variety, while avoiding a position of parti pris *in favor of any contemporary movement or direction. No serious critic would deny the value of labels in studying modern art; the danger is that we shall come to trust too much in the limiting dogmas to which these labels are affixed. It seems to me that we pre-empt a function of history when we attempt to decide unreservedly what kinds of art are truly "modern" and what are static or reactionary. As mentioned in one of the following chapters, the story of Ingres is a case in point. Considered a fussy obstructionist by the rebels of his day, he has been hailed as a revolutionary, along with Cézanne and Seurat, by such pioneers of contemporary art as the cubists and the purists. An underlying premise of this book is that, even from an advanced viewpoint, the romantic-realist Hopper is as valid a subject for study as Soutine the expressionist. And I speak now not only of intrinsic quality, but of possible meaning for later generations of painters. We are not going to settle in our time the direction art* must *take; now, as always, good painters will follow divergent paths to conflicting yet equally rewarding goals.*

J.T.S.

THREE AMERICAN WATERCOLORISTS: I. CHARLES DEMUTH

Cubism as invented by Picasso and Braque was a sombre, formal and disciplined language. Later it became more colorful and free, but an American artist, Charles Demuth, was able to prove that cubism could speak in whispers with extraordinary wit and delicacy, a special idiom of the murmured aside. He understood the exact strength of fragility, and in his watercolors he remains, to my mind, one of the finest artists our century and country have produced.

Demuth was born in 1883 in Lancaster, Pennsylvania, and lived there nearly all his life in the old brick house where he was born. His art reflects this security and permanence, not in its subject matter so much as in its subtle, aristocratic air of sanctuary and withdrawal. One sometimes senses in his work the absolute negation of Whitman's proud boast, "I was the man, I suffered, I was there." Demuth was an artist, he was tormented by incurable illness, but he mostly stayed at home in Lancaster or Provincetown and waited for experience to come to him, his imagination an exquisite trap, fixed, waiting, exerting an enormous power of attraction. If we compare his watercolors with those of "Pop" Hart, who went everywhere to wring life by the hand, Demuth's essential detachment becomes clear. It is no accident that he revered Proust and dreamed of illustrating his works; his own psychology was Proustian; his life centered in his room, and he recalled or imagined there everything needed for his art. And because he did not chase after sensation, his art is never out of breath. It has the relaxed yet sharp manners of genius at home, protected and certain and free of strenuous pose.

Demuth was trained under Thomas Anshutz at the Pennsylvania Academy of Fine Arts, where William M. Chase and Henry McCarter were also instructors. The role of Philadelphia in forming his taste must have been important. For that city has bred in certain modern artists an urbanity quite different from that imposed by New York, where painters are so often inspired by aspects of the local scene or turn convulsively inward toward expressionism. Beginning with "The Eight," Philadelphia has, of course, lost many of its leading painters to Manhattan. There has nevertheless developed at the hands of its faithful what might with reservations be called a Philadelphian art, a painting which shows close sympathy for the traditions running from Mannerism to the Rococo, which proclaims Grand Style heritage and holds apart in some degree from the modern constriction of iconographic aim. From Demuth to Franklin Watkins to young Walter Stuempfig, a line of descent may be traced; its basic characteristic is gracious stylistic invention as differentiated from the blunt declamation lately so common in American painting as a whole. The virtues of modern Philadelphian art, if we may call it that, are by no means minor or artificial; within the leeway of certain exceptions, they are, however, more or less distinctive.

In 1904 Demuth went to Paris for two years and returned there in 1912, at which latter time he enrolled in the *Académie Colarossi* and remained until 1914. We know little regarding his development during the first of these trips, but he came home from the second fully equipped for the brilliant career which lay ahead. In Paris he was exposed to cubism, ever afterwards an important instrument in his technical equipment. But after he returned home, his lasting regard for cubism was qualified in the direction of ironic detachment by his friendship for Marcel Duchamp, most sophisticated member of the cubist circle, who arrived in this country during the First World War. Duchamp had already brought to cubism a metaphysical enrichment; his pictures complicated the architectonics of Picasso and Braque through enigmatic purport and a sense of mockery. In a manner of speaking, he had hung a magnet in the middle of the pure cubist temple to see what it would attract blindly; he had proclaimed the validity of the accidents of external appearances and inner reverie, the accrual of philosophic meaning to abstract form. His influence on Demuth was immense. To it may partially be traced Demuth's use of provocative titles, his devotion to agility as opposed to weight, his choice of the alert over the solemn, the fugitive over the placid, his elegance and disdain.

Even without Duchamp's example, Demuth would almost certainly have found his own track. His excitement at the discovery of cubism was great, but his taste did not then forever freeze and point, as did that of so many lesser figures of the decade 1910–20. Instead, like another American painter of his period, Lyonel Feininger, he was vitalized as an artist by the very disparity of his sources. Working in Germany, Feininger found in the nineteenth-century German Romantic, Caspar David Friedrich, a means of restoring to cubism the emotion and mood which its inaugurators had usually played down or excluded. Demuth, on the other hand, turned to an artist equally removed from the cubist premise, but in a different direction — Honoré Fragonard, whose rosy colors and deft gaiety might seem totally irreconcilable with cubism but in Demuth's hands were not. Thus the two Americans found their separate methods of giving cubism new life: Feininger by blowing into its mouth a romantic air; Demuth by slapping it smartly on the back.

A regard for the eighteenth century was an essential of Demuth's vision, though it was by no means exclusive, as will appear. And perhaps this regard may be understood at its clearest in the architectural subjects to which he first turned during a trip to Bermuda in 1917. These pictures, as Alfred Barr has pointed out, are comparable to Feininger's works in their gossamer refinement and romanticism of atmosphere. But while Feininger's enthusiasm was for the Gothic style, Demuth recaptured the echoing proportions and topographical precision of seventeenth and eighteenth-century architectural studies (page 13). Feininger deeply admired the German Middle Ages and the Baltic Gothicism of Friedrich; Demuth favored Sir Christopher Wren and those adaptations of his style which recur in Colonial buildings. It is true that Demuth sometimes painted modern industrial scenes, as in *Aucassin and Nicolette, End of the Parade* and *The Piano Mover's Holiday.* But even these he portrayed with a lyric nicety which relates them

Charles DEMUTH: In Vaudeville, 1918. *Watercolor, 11 x 8". Collection Mr. and Mrs. Samuel S. White, III, Philadelphia.*

spiritually to the eighteenth-century factories of Joseph Wright of Derby rather than to those of Demuth's own contemporaries, Charles Sheeler and Preston Dickinson.

During his lifetime, Demuth was often grouped with Sheeler and Dickinson as one of the so-called "Immaculates," who made sharp cleanliness of technique a guiding principle. Yet unlike them he never quite accepted machine-forms as objects for reverent emulation. If, for example, we compare Demuth's *Paquebot, Paris* of 1917 (the first of his industrial subjects) with Sheeler's famous *Upper Deck,* we discover a fundamental divergence in approach. Demuth's picture is an abstract design not entirely dissimilar to those produced by the eighteenth-century French architect, C. N. Ledoux; it conveys little sense of mechanical function. Sheeler's image, contrarily, records in detail and with open admiration the polished intricacies of modern engineering. His machines and factories *work,* while Demuth's seem to have caught his interest because in them survives something of the architectural clarity of a pre-industrial time.

Soon after his return from Paris in 1914, Demuth began to paint figure pieces in watercolor. These works may be divided into two rough categories: those in which illustrative detail plays an important part, among them his interpretations of favorite authors; and those which by comparison are formally organized.

He appears to have used the two styles in alternation rather than to have progressed from one to the other. His "illustrative" style reveals that in matters of decoration and literary inspiration he preferred the nineteenth century quite as pointedly as in architecture he favored the seventeenth and eighteenth. None of his paintings of architectural façades, so far as I know, depicts the gloomy, brave heritage of our post-bellum past which has engrossed men like Charles Burchfield and Edward Hopper. But in his interiors with figures, Demuth's predilection for the Victorian era's robust furniture and fanciful bric-a-brac is evident, and it is worth noting that his own house in Lancaster was decorated with late nineteenth-century pieces long before the current vogue for them began. As to his literary tastes, the dates of the books he illustrated make clear his devotion to the century before his own: Balzac's *La Fille Aux Yeux d'Or* (1835); Zola's *L'Assommoir* (1877) and *Nana* (1880); Poe's *Masque of the Red Death* (1842); Henry James's *The Turn of the Screw* (1898); Frank Wedekind's *Erdgeist* (1895).

Granted their nineteenth-century subject matter, one might expect that his illustrative works would be influenced by the art of Aubrey Beardsley and Toulouse-Lautrec: they were indeed, and Demuth worshipped both artists. The example of Beardsley and Lautrec perhaps accounts for Demuth's flirtation with a decadence about which he was never wholly serious, and it may be traced in certain *art nouveau* mannerisms which recur in his illustrative watercolors. But the same influence is also apparent in Demuth's more formal works, to which Beardsley's clean silhouettes and Lautrec's superb handling of broad masses contributed importantly. Time and again in viewing Demuth's figure pieces a *fin de siècle* reminiscence suggests itself — an attenuated shoe and foot out of Beardsley, a woman's profile drawn with Lautrec's jagged, incisive contours. Yet Demuth was able to assimilate and make his own even these vigorous sources, partly because of his own decided originality and partly because of the very cultivation of his taste. If we cross cubism with Fragonard and cross it again with Beardsley-Lautrec, we may approximate the superficial character of Demuth's art. But we shall fail to define its personal substance and intensely private nature.

Demuth's illustrative works, notably his interpretations of Henry James's *The Turn of the Screw* and *The Beast in the Jungle,* made apparently for his own pleasure rather than

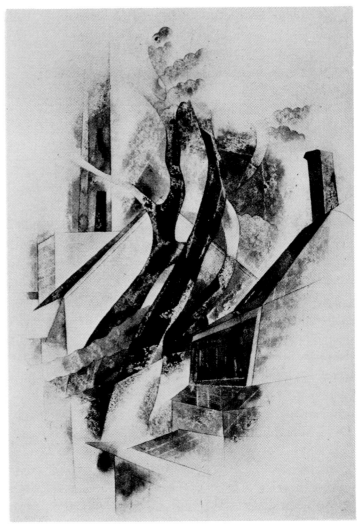

Charles DEMUTH: Houses, 1918. *Watercolor, 13¾ x 9¾". Colum-bus Gallery of Fine Arts, Ferdinand Howald Collection.*

with an eye to publication, have long been regarded as among his finest watercolors. Their fame is deserved, but he seems to me to have been a greater artist in the figure pieces of 1917–19 which depict vaudeville and nightclub performers without reference to literary source (page 11). There is an added strength in these, and the structural function of color is more imaginatively realized. In nearly all his watercolors, Demuth appears to have overlaid color on an image more or less completely drawn in pencil. In the series of vaudeville acrobats, however, color is far more than a surface tinting, how-ever brilliant. It adds depth to the nervous meanderings of line. In the *Acrobats* (page 15), for example, color is used with extraordinary variety and skill. On the legs of the cyclists, watercolor is applied film over film, with wonderful control of shading and transparency and a perfect mastery of the tonal resonance of black. The freer wash handling of the stage and backdrop provides a radiant foil to the figures. And to the remarkable figure "8" pattern against which the acrobats are placed, color supplies a rare intensity. This passage reminds us that if Fragonard was at the heart of Demuth's love for the eighteenth century, another of his idols was William Blake. Quite possibly Demuth's frequent use of rounded forms owes something to Fragonard, for whom the garland was so irresistible a motif, who often vignetted his figures by circular openings in hedge or drapery. Yet in the *Acrobats* and other Demuth figure pieces of 1917–19, there is much of the heady power of Blake. Demuth's sprightliness is Rococo, but his vigor has an almost mystical impetus, as if Blake's devout compression were never lost to mind. There is, indeed, a decided affinity between such a work as the *Acrobats* and Blake's "The Worshipper of Reason" from *The Song of Los;* one is godless godchild to the other; both use abstract design as a psychological, no less than as a formal, accompaniment to figures.

In many of Demuth's figure pieces there is an emphasis on intricacy of balance, on those daring relationships of stance and muscular action which so delighted him in performances by acrobats and dancers. At times his art seems altogether Mannerist in its tensions and exaggerations of contour, and he was particularly fond of the "C" curve formed by the figure of one acrobat arched outward from another, the whole framed by complementary arcs of color. Significantly, the title of Demuth's longest article on painting is "Across a Greco Is Written," wherein he pays tribute to El Greco, Rubens, Watteau, Blake and Beardsley — all of whom stemmed in varying degrees from the Mannerist tradition. To their company might be added Fragonard, whose *Le Verrou* and other works often depict the kind of choreographic interaction in which Demuth was vitally interested. The bulge of muscles is a further Mannerist device in Demuth's art; the young athletic male is his usual protagonist. But he created out of distortion, unbalance and violent motion an imagery of exceptional force and cohesion, believable, witty, with superb carrying power for work executed in watercolor on so small a scale. And his Mannerism at times derived a rather bitter contemporary liveliness from his acute observation, his sense of climax in the memories he brought home to Lancaster and slowly reworked.

With the exception of a few watercolors painted toward the end of his life, all of Demuth's figure pieces were completed before 1920, a fact which makes the more astonishing their variety and richness of invention. After that date, as he confessed to Henry McBride, the artist no longer had the strength for such subjects and mostly painted flowers instead. If his interpretations of literature were intended for himself, his acrobats and other figures for a special and devoted following, his flower pieces were in a sense ready-made for the museums. Their technical acumen is masterly, their sensitivity so marked that they belonged almost as soon as they were done to an unquestioned place in native watercolor art. Occasionally, it must be admitted, they fall off into coldness and

Charles DEMUTH: Acrobats, 1919. *Watercolor, 13 x 7⅞". The Museum of Modern Art, New York.*

over-refinement, and their very precision becomes listless, as though Demuth's tragic ill health allowed him his full power only part of the time. But at their best their purity has its own quick pulse, their forms are large and vigorous, their boldness comparable to that of his best figures. And on the whole it may be said that almost none of his watercolors is banal and few are weak, so that Demuth assuredly deserves his position as one of the classics of modern American painting. He was, perhaps, our only dandy of genius since Whistler.

If a poll were conducted among qualified Americans as to the finest of our living painters, the reply might not be unanimous, but it would probably favor John Marin. On the
other hand, if a like poll were held among Europeans reasonably conversant with living
American art, Marin's name would appear well down the list. At least we may assume it
would, judging by the indifferent opinion of his work so often expressed by foreign
critics and amateurs. In this country we think of Marin as one of the finest watercolorists
we have ever produced. Some of us — I am reluctantly not of this number — consider
him a major oil painter as well. To Europeans, contrarily, he seems a minor expressionist,
fresh in color and style, but lacking in inventive capacity and limited in scale. This is
a rather paradoxical situation, for we might expect critics abroad to appreciate Marin for
certain virtues which are readily understood in Europe: his sensual relish of medium;
his pictorial warmth and daring. The truth seems to be, however, that Marin is one of
those artists who does not transplant particularly well, and in this he may be compared to
such painters as Giorgio Morandi in Italy and Matthew Smith in England — men who
are regarded at home as far superior to artists from those countries whom we know
fairly well here and admire.

In Marin's case this is very likely a temporary state of affairs, and I believe that Europeans will eventually see in him many of the qualities we now see, though perhaps with
changed emphasis. Meanwhile, the difference of opinion as to Marin's stature can be
accounted for primarily by our closer familiarity with his art. There are, however, some
secondary factors which may be mentioned here, not at all as derogation, but simply
as explanation.

To begin with, Marin fits perfectly an ingrained, romantic American image of the
gifted Yankee, laconic, profound, fiercely independent, honest, gentle and proud. "His
letters as well as his speech," Loren Mozley has written, "are full of tasty Yankee expressions such as 'Cracker-jack,' 'High Cockalorum,' 'Hum-Dinger.'" A man of immense dignity, his simple, strong, weather-beaten personality has made him an impressive figure in American cultural life, even though he lives in relative seclusion in New
Jersey or Maine, and has made no effort to utilize personal charm as an asset in his career.
A decisive factor in the creation of his great reputation was his long association with
Alfred Stieglitz. For nearly forty years (1909–46) the American public was given a
chance to see Marin's work at Stieglitz's various galleries, sometimes annually and sometimes oftener. And during these many years Stieglitz was on hand to praise and defend
his friend's pictures, assuring them a mounting prestige. Of course Stieglitz's role in
Marin's career was far greater than this; indeed, to him must be given much of the credit
for the fact that Marin seems to have realized his gifts as completely as any American

John MARIN: Maine Islands, 1922. *Watercolor, 16½ x 19½". Phillips Memorial Gallery, Washington,* D.C.

artist, living or dead. In any case, the Marin-Stieglitz combination, with its incorruptible purity and devotion, worked well in awakening public response, and gradually Marin came to be accepted by large numbers of people as the best of our living painters. His slow, sometimes painful, but always steady ascent was owing primarily — let me repeat — to the strength and authenticity of his talent. A contributory factor, however, was that he and his art reflect a deep native faith in a strident, clean, irresistible energy peculiar to the American heritage and to contemporary American life. We are helped to admire certain artists by their unlocalized idiosyncrasy; others touch in us a national chord, and Marin is among them.

It was to the fierce power of urban life in America that Marin first responded, and quite naturally, since he had been trained as an architect and had practised as one briefly.

17

From 1905 to 1911 he lived abroad, except for the years 1909–10, and produced a number of etchings of European architecture, working in the Whistlerian style. But an explosive force was building within him. We sense it gathering, at its very beginning, in the agitated handling of the sky in an etching of 1909, *Notre Dame Seen from the Quai Célestins.* He is calmer again in his famous print of Chartres Cathedral, executed the following year, where the lines are reverent and careful. Just the same, this etching has a curious vibrancy, not unlike that in certain prints by James Ensor, which Marin had almost certainly not seen.

In 1911 Marin returned home permanently, and was caught up in the extraordinary excitement as to modern expressive means which centered here in Stieglitz's gallery, "291." He began very soon to abandon his concern with the formal properties of architecture and to show instead a new and romantic interest in architecture's humanistic purport. "Are the buildings themselves dead?" he wrote Stieglitz in 1913, referring to the skyscrapers of New York. "You cannot create a work of art unless the things you behold respond to something within you. Therefore if these buildings move me, they too must have life. Thus the whole city is alive; buildings, people, all are alive; and the more they move me the more I feel them to be alive."

It is easy now, when New York City appears overdeveloped, to dismiss Marin's statement as ingenuously mystic, or belatedly Whitmanesque. But the period preceding the First World War was one of exceptional vitality in New York's growth, and in any case the pictorial result of Marin's attitude remains unqualifiedly impressive. Between 1911 and 1913 he produced a series of etchings of Brooklyn Bridge and the Woolworth Building. These announce his mature structural style — a style of toppling verticals, zig-zag planes, staccato accents and expressionist whorls. His handling of color developed simultaneously, in a parallel direction. As early as 1910, in watercolors of the Tyrol, he had attained that remarkable control of translucence which has remained one of his most distinguished characteristics. For the most part in this series he had let his color run free, as Kandinsky was doing at the time, and very often it fell into rounded or flowing patterns, fairly unrestrained. But then in a watercolor entitled *The Mountain Tyrol,* one notices that a grove of trees supplies a triangular base to the composition, giving a cornucopia effect and introducing that schematic tension so frequently felt in later works. In 1912, back in New York, he painted such pictures as the *Bridge with New York Skyline* and *Woolworth Building, No. 31.* With these watercolors he found the way he has since developed, but never fundamentally altered.

His colors now tended to congeal into crystal forms, some sharply edged, others half melted and moving. He developed over the ten years from 1912 to 1922 most of the basic compositional formulas within which he was to maintain to a remarkable degree the elements of freshness and surprise. Many of his watercolors of that decade give the illusion of opening out from or closing in on a circular core, like iris diaphragms in which peaked forms combine closely to create round. Equally often, however, the structure is predominantly vertical or horizontal and follows the pattern not of a cogwheel, but of

John MARIN: Lower Manhattan, 1922. *Watercolor, 21⅝ x 26⅞". The Museum of Modern Art, New York.*

a fitful sea. Again, he plays vigorous circular motifs against solid, ruled masses, as in his brilliant pictures of sunsets with bold horizons. Finally, he occasionally combines these three more or less separate formulas into an unpredictable whole, using elements from each.

A basic ingredient of his art remains the abstracted cone, zigzag, rectangle or square, and it is natural that he should often have been compared to the cubists by whom, particularly on his return to America in 1911, he was undeniably affected. Yet there is, I think, a fundamental divergence between Marin's approach and that of the cubists. For whereas Picasso and Braque had used cubism's forms as a considered, overall structure, at first analytic and later synthetic, Marin has used comparable abstract stylizations either as vehicles of emotional proclamation or as simpler surface ornament, meant to beguile the eye. And here we come on a divisibility in Marin's art which is seldom stressed. There is Marin the expressionist poet, full of convinced, headlong lyricism to the very borders of his watercolors, a man who records an overwhelming impression, without pause, with rare and piercing sensitivity. This is the Marin of the *Lower Manhattan* series of 1920–22 (page 19), of the superbly immediate responses to the New Mexico landscape and to the Maine Coast (page 17) ; it is, to my mind, the greatest Marin. There is also a more relaxed Marin, who takes the components of his vision out of their compulsive sequence, so to speak, and rearranges them in a more purely ornamental order. This is the Marin of the circus pictures and the nudes, the man who sometimes carves and tints his own frames, who unlinks his abstract forms and pastes them up more or less separately as a decorative frieze surrounding a central image. At times this Marin works with magnificent sureness and flourish, yet on the whole we miss in his decorative paintings the heady impetus of those watercolors in which he is carried away from start to finish by a single fiery inspiration.

Perhaps there is a third Marin to be considered as well, for he occasionally seems interested in the kind of direct reportage at which his contemporary, "Pop" Hart, was a specialist. As early as 1908, in *London Omnibus,* he had completed a watercolor whose broad, "impressionist" technique does not entirely obscure a lively interest in particulars of characterization. Since that date a realistic strain (in the conventional meaning of the term) has appeared at intervals in his art. It is never allowed to provide the central theme or to become anecdotal. Nevertheless, there are Marin watercolors of New York's streets or of the circus in which the expressionist mood is tempered by an interest in details of local color. Everyone who knows his art well will remember certain pictures in which he seems to squint a little instead of staring with blazing eyes. The paintings to which I refer are more impressive on the whole than those in his decorative vein. But it seems to me that he is incomparable only when his emotion pours out with hasty violence, when he improvises on universals like city streets, the sun, the mountains, the rocks and the sea.

To divide Marin's art into categories is not, of course, to explain its quality. This quality is primarily impetuous; it springs from a sensibility so acute, burning at so consuming a heat, that it finds its logical expression in watercolor, I think. Corrections and revisions do Marin little good, for he is right or wrong to begin with, and once begun he must translate his vision quickly. In any case, his best watercolors have an inner illumination, a textural excitement and a sureness of stroke which tend to disappear in many of his oils. Nor does the heavier pigment always give him an added richness. If, for example, one has seen at the Duncan Phillips Gallery in Washington a Marin oil and a Soutine hanging in adjoining galleries, a comparison suggests itself. While Soutine used every physical property of the oil medium to achieve a luxurious variety of tonal effect and an accompanying psychical intensity, Marin's picture, though of good quality, seems unnecessarily labored and at the same time hesitant. Only when one comes on the great Marin watercolors at the Phillips Gallery does one realize that his expressionism is as forceful as Soutine's — the sharp, clear cry as penetrating emotionally as the Lithuanian's thrashing torment.

The art of Marin is more difficult to describe in words than that of any other living American artist. Perhaps this is because of its visual directness, its all-satisfying claim on the eye. There are many modern pictures whose forms we carry with us as a submerged part of memory, and whose qualities are confirmed rather than revealed afresh on later seeing. This is true not only of so-called "literary" paintings or of those with decided associational values, but of many totally abstract works. With Marin our experience is quite different — at least mine is. We recognize him at once as an American, as I suggested at the beginning of this chapter, and this is unquestionably a help toward cordiality. Yet we recognize his full value anew each time, and at his best he is always more rewarding and inspired than we had remembered, no matter how recently we have seen his work or how well we have known it. He is unmistakably an American artist, yes, but there is perhaps no one else among our modern painters so subtle and renewable in appeal, so instantly and unpredictably the master of our senses.

THREE AMERICAN WATERCOLORISTS: III. CHARLES BURCHFIELD

In February, 1944, the University of Buffalo, New York, awarded its Chancellor's Medal to Charles Burchfield, artist. The University's citation was altogether exceptional in understanding and humility, and I should like to repeat part of it here. The medal was given to Burchfield "in recognition of the fact that through his convincing revelation of the beauty latent in familiar surroundings he has attained eminence among the painters of his generation and has dignified Buffalo in the eyes of the world." How touching, even if repeated by custom for this award, are the words "dignified Buffalo in the eyes of the world!" How remarkable that an American community should go beyond its more obvious sources of pride and admit that a living artist had brought it spiritual stature! The citation came from a university, of course, but it came from one at which local influence is strong, so that we may accept it as reflecting in some degree the sentiment of the city. The use of the word "dignified" is exceptionally telling; it brings honor to Buffalo, its University, the artist and the nation.

The words of the citation are all true. It is Burchfield's inspired handling of commonplace American subject matter which has earned him his esteemed place in modern art, and since 1921 he has found a majority of his themes in Buffalo or in the nearby towns and countryside. But the citation is the more commendable in that Burchfield has not flattered the local scene except in the sense of having celebrated a beauty on which the cultured citizenry of Buffalo whenever possible has turned its back — the lively squalor of railroad yards and factory areas, Victorian streets whose imaginative architecture the rich have abandoned to the poor, preferring the reactionary "modernism" of the Colonial and rustic European styles. Burchfield very frequently paints what the average American community has left behind or hopes to improve beyond recognition; his art depicts not civic progress but a potential civic remorse, not enterprise but nostalgia and regret. So far as his watercolors of the city are concerned, he is a painter of memories in an era of anticipation.

All honor, then, to Buffalo's University. And there is yet another award to be made Burchfield one day, this time by the town of Salem, Ohio, where the artist grew up and where, between 1916 and 1918, he painted one of the great series of American watercolors. In the former year he moved to New York for two months, hoping to discover an individual style after long technical training under Henry G. Keller at the Cleveland School of Art. He experienced instead the most violent homesickness for Ohio, and fled back to his old job as an accountant in Salem. If he had not returned home, if his watercolors of 1916–18 had been painted in New York, we might ascribe the quality of his early period to a consuming nostalgia for home, compelling him to an imaginative re-creation of familiar scenes, as in the case of Giorgio de Chirico during his Paris years, 1911–15, or of Marc Chagall over a roughly comparable period in the French capital. But Burchfield went back to Salem. There, as he later declared, he was at first unhappy — "A curious mental depression assailed me, and I worked constantly to keep it down." He knew that Salem was where he belonged, but perhaps he knew as well, in despair, that the chances were remote of his producing in that isolation the art he hoped for. New York had not held him, and he was home as a man of twenty-three in a provincial midwestern town, drawn there by memories of childhood too strong to withstand. He proceeded to intensify these memories in his paintings, as justification of himself, as refuge from his uneventful existence, as a token of struggle after the surrender of homecoming. How magnificently he succeeded, is attested by the watercolors he completed during the two years before his induction into the Army in 1918. Nothing in recent American art seems more directly wrenched out of inner experience, nothing more acutely felt or passionately stated, more original or truly creative.

It seems incredible that Burchfield could have produced his early watercolors without some knowledge of the European romantic tradition, particularly that of the Englishmen, Blake and Samuel Palmer. But such is the fact. Nor did he know anything of advanced contemporary art in America or abroad. His *Insects at Twilight* of 1917 is comparable to many paintings by Paul Klee in its visual suggestion of witching vibrations of sound, yet Burchfield had never heard of Klee, and was almost totally different in personal character. While Klee's conception of nature often took its point of departure from the naturalist's cabinet — from the curious entomological or botanical specimen brought home and examined in isolation — Burchfield roamed the fields remembered from boyhood and retained an elemental sense of the outdoors: in his art direct, large-scale forces of wind and light replace the enchanted laboratory slides of Klee. Burchfield also had not heard of the expressionist movement in Europe. But his leopard trees, his bat-like, grimacing flowers, his looping branches and tentacled clouds are organized with the broad, summary power of the German artists of *Die Brücke* (The Bridge) and *Der Blaue Reiter* (The Blue Rider). He knew nothing really except Ohio and his childhood there, but these he knew with extraordinary perception.

Despite the depression of mind to which the artist has referred, his first Salem watercolors were relatively serene in spirit. The *Cat-Tails* and *Rogues' Gallery* of 1916 recall Japanese prints in their delicacy of line and use of silhouette. The second is probably slightly later than the first, and already the forms have turned animistic; soon flowers and trees will become protagonists of strong drama. By 1917 Burchfield's vision had become more macabre and fevered — "As I progressed . . . I went further back into childhood memories and it became such an obsession that a decadence set in. I tried to re-create such moods as fear of the dark, the feelings of flowers before a storm, and even to visualize the songs of insects and other sounds. While perhaps most of these things had meaning only for me, I think that through them I developed a primitive outlook that became a basis for all my future work. . . ."

This statement by the artist was made in 1928, a year before his early watercolors were discovered by Edward W. Root and two years before an exhibition at the Museum of Modern Art in New York brought them to public and enthusiastic notice. Probably this fact accounts for the apologetic tone of Burchfield's comment; he had done the Salem watercolors a long time ago, and he thought of them as essentially private. But what he described as "decadence" was actually a deepening of mood. And contrary to the modest opinion he gave of them in 1928, his watercolors of 1917–18 belong now to the most universal realm of American romantic art, and constitute a youthful foil to the older-age idyllicism of Albert Pinkham Ryder.

If we consider, for example, such well-known works as *Church Bells Ringing — Rainy Winter Night* (page 25) and *The Night Wind,* we are confronted with great originality and an amazing aptitude for visual rhythms. The spirit of these watercolors is eighteenth-century "Gothick," that is to say, their introspection is morbidly apprehensive; they keep an excited tryst with imagined horror. But whereas the weather in "Gothick" painting and prose was frequently as artificial as the "ruined" architecture, here it strikes hard; the terror of the elements is physically as well as nervously real. Occasionally, as in *Garden of Memories,* Burchfield worked in a more illustrative "Gothick" style, conveying a sinister portent by repeating in the windows and clapboards of the house, in the surrounding flowers, even in the eyebrows of the dreaming old woman, the zigzag form which I have previously described as bat-like. In *Church Bells Ringing,* on the other hand, the very motion of the image provides a menacing power, and one recalls T. S. Eliot's "Rhapsody on a Windy Night" —

Midnight shakes the memory
As a madman shakes a dead geranium.

The church steeple trembles violently in the ominous wind, and the houses shake from its clangor. The sense of motion described is not kinetic, as it was with the futurists; it seems instead a direct translation of emotional seizure in the child mind. Describing the picture some years later, Burchfield wrote: "It was an attempt to express a child-hood emotion — a rainy winter night — the churchbell is ringing and it terrifies me (the child) — the bell-ringing motive reaches out and saturates the rainy sky — the roofs of the houses dripping with rain are influenced; the child attempts to be com-forted by the thoughts of candle lights and Christmas trees, but the fear of the black, rainy night is overpowering . . ." The thoughts with which the child tries to soothe its anguish are imprinted on the façade of the house at the left, but are blurred by the storm. They cannot in any case be approached, since overhead the steeple hovers like a malignant bird, while pools lie like snakes in the street, and the façade of a second house is dark with nameless patterns of terror.

How eloquent an image this is! That it was produced in Salem, Ohio, by a young and inexperienced artist is one of the phenomena of modern American art. Indeed, if Burch-field had produced nothing but this and his other watercolors of 1916–18, he would be entitled to a lasting place among our most imaginative painters. But so consuming an inspiration could not last for long, and presently the brief spell was broken by the artist's service in the Army.

When he returned to civilian life in 1918, Burchfield took up watercolor again, but he was dissatisfied with what he produced and destroyed it. His period of military serv-ice had been short and uneventful compared to Stanley Spencer's (see page 125), but like the English artist he came home to a town which had lost its power to inspire him through childhood associations. In 1919 he began to work in a new, more objective direction, and from that year until 1921, when he moved to Buffalo, he struggled to adjust cooling introspective emotion to a rising interest in the American scene for its own sake. Few watercolors of these two years survive, probably not more than a half dozen, of which only one seems to be dated 1919. Yet among them are some of his loveliest works. The dated watercolor, for example, shows freight cars on a railroad siding in winter (page 27). If there is in it none of the mystical excitement of Burch-field's Salem period, it would be difficult to think of many American watercolors in which there is so memorable a warmth and luminosity, as if it were painted on velvet with the most luxurious of dyes. Moreover, the image is more subtly stylized than its apparent realism lets us realize at first glance. The sides and wheels of the railroad cars are rendered with Oriental economy of stroke and great variety of pattern; the land-scape and telegraph pole are freely distorted for emotive effect.

After he moved to Buffalo in 1921, Burchfield's attention was attracted by the post-Civil War architecture which survives there in such abundance. He continued to paint landscapes, but many of these seem formally romantic and cold, while his architectural watercolors sounded a new note in modern American painting: the pictorial re-creation of this country's immediate past in architecture. Indeed, Victorian architecture became

Charles BURCHFIELD: Church Bells Ringing—Rainy Winter Night, 1917. *Watercolor, 30 x 19". Collection Mrs. Louise M. Dunn, Cleveland.*

for Burchfield the same focal point for nostalgic mood that the abbeys of the Middle Ages had been for the romantics of the eighteenth and early nineteenth centuries. So drastic a compression of centuries into decades, for purposes of romantic-historical appeal, is part of the American tradition. It was this same compression which led Washington Irving to begin one of his most famous tales: "In this by-place of nature, there abode, in a remote period of American history, that is to say, some thirty years since, a worthy wight of the name of Ichabod Crane."

In his treatment of post-bellum architecture Burchfield is usually described as a satirist. But if he is that, his satire is based on sympathy rather than bitterness. "Things that are not done out of love, will not last," he told E. P. Richardson a few years ago. "There is not a thing in this exhibit [the large Burchfield retrospective exhibition at the Albright Art Gallery in Buffalo, held in 1944] that I was not enthusiastic about, that I did not like when I painted it. I am not a satirist. I have had to live that down all my life . . . I remember that I once did a picture of a wooden store with a false front. I thought it was just kind of interesting — it seemed very American to me and I liked it. But in New York everybody thought it was a satire."

Occasionally, as in the much-exhibited *Promenade* of 1927–28, he has included a note of humorous fantasy, in this case typified by the train of mongrels which stalks a dowdy woman and her bundled lap dog. Yet even here the satiric content is dominated by the attendant, warm rendering of a late century "Italian" villa and its mansarded neighbor. Moreover, the frequent critical emphasis on Burchfield's satire disregards the fact that late Victorian architecture suits both his macabre turn of mind and his instinctive visual predilections. In painting American architecture of the 1870's and 1880's, the artist has nearly always heightened its "Gothick" weirdness through subjective handling of details, as a comparison between his watercolors and photographs of their subjects made clear in a recent issue of *Art News*. To a painter who had previously depicted swirling symbols of childhood fear, the turgid exuberance and beetled, fanciful trim of late nineteenth-century American architecture must have been naturally appealing.

Viewed purely as documents, Burchfield's watercolors of Buffalo are invaluable Americana. The best of them are much more than that; the least fall into a genre formula which is often too consciously picturesque. But nearly all his works are notable for the sensitivity to weather which I have already mentioned and which Burchfield describes as one of his main preoccupations. He prefers to work in certain months — November, March and August — and his inspiration varies with the season and light; he finds particular excitement in gray days of rain and the hard, still melancholy of winter. His naturalism is self-contained, and he finds it impossible to use photographs as preparatory material, declaring that they would impede the subconscious changes he makes in working from a given scene. He is not a humanist like Ben Shahn, for whom photographs of figures in action have provided an intimate and valuable link with reality. Burchfield paints a world in which man is merely the casual inhabitant of his own creations —

Charles BURCHFIELD: Freight Cars, 1919. *Watercolor, 11½ x 19⅝". Collection Alfred H. Barr, Jr., New York.*

architecture and the cultivated landscape. Light lives in his houses, and shadows rather than people; the windows are closed, or they open to make their own wry face.

Very recently Burchfield has turned back to the works of his Salem period, and has attempted to bring to fruition on a larger scale images which he had conceived nearly thirty years before. In some cases he has actually enlarged earlier works by the addition of borders; in others, he has made bigger copies. The painter's attempt to revisit his youth, to regain its freshness and add a more mature skill, is an extremely interesting experiment. Perhaps it will yet succeed or lead to a totally new expression. One can only record for now that the completed watercolors of this series seem swollen ghosts of the Salem masterpieces; perhaps the most successful is a picture begun entirely anew, without direct reference to his early period, though in its spirit. In any case, we can be thankful to Burchfield for his astonishing visions of 1916–18 and for the best of his interpretations of the Buffalo area. He was precocious to begin with, and he is still younger than most American artists of comparable eminence. We can await his further development with interest and hope.

MAX WEBER AND EDWARD HOPPER

No two contemporary American painters furnish a more absolute contrast than Max Weber and Edward Hopper. Consider, to begin with, their different heritages. Weber was born in 1881 at Vialostok in Russia, and came to this country with his family at the age of ten, already imbued with the psychological flavor of Central and Eastern Europe, where our century's expressionism has had its most tenacious roots. Hopper, on the other hand, was born in 1882 across the river from New York City in Nyack, a small American town whose horizontality of plan remains an earmark of his compositions, whose Victorian architecture is a main artery of his romanticism, whose aggressive modern façade acts as backdrop to his realism. In nineteenth-century Vialostok, Weber grew up in an atmosphere of rich legend, mournful ritual and relieving splendor of costume, ornament and gesture. Nyack offered Hopper a plainer but hardy nourishment in youth: his middle-class, small-town upbringing must account in part for the solemnity, reticence and blunt evaluation of appearances which characterize his mature art.

As a young man Weber traveled to Madrid to study El Greco, to Italy where Giotto, Masaccio, Piero della Francesca, Signorelli and Mantegna were revealed to him in their full power. Later, in 1908, he went to the Low Countries to see the masterpieces of the fifteenth, sixteenth and seventeenth centuries. Moreover, he matured in the very center of the contemporary revolution in art. He was in Paris from the autumn of 1905 to December 1908, so that he was a near and enthusiastic witness to the breaking through of vigorous, insurgent forces in painting. He saw the work of the *fauves;* he was a pupil of Matisse; he attended the exhibitions of Cézanne which established that master as the prophet of a new structural emphasis; he became an intimate friend of the *Douanier* Rousseau, whose emotional freshness has contributed so much to modern art. And all the while Weber was developing under the impact of a tremendously fertile period in esthetic re-evaluation, a period in which the body of art was newly measured, so to speak, just as later its psychology was analysed in contemporary terms by the surrealists and their associates. Like the advanced Parisian artists who were his friends, Weber was enormously excited by the expressive capacity of remote, alien or untutored arts — Far and Near Eastern painting and textiles, the tribal sculpture of Africa and the Americas. At the early time in our century, art went around the world in eighty months, and Weber went with it.

Holger Cahill in his excellent monograph on the artist declares that Weber has lived the history of modern art in America. To which might be added that Weber has lived the history of modern art in Europe as well. It is, therefore, no wonder that he seems the most European of our living artists. In saying this I do not refer primarily to his closeness of sympathy with movements originating abroad, though with the single and brief ex-

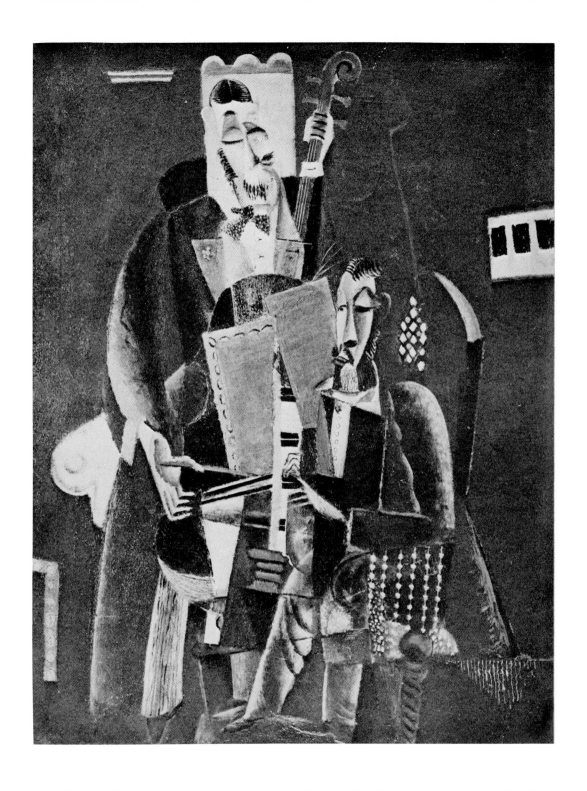

Max WEBER: The Two Musicians, (1917). *Oil, 40⅛ x 30⅛". The Museum of Modern Art, N.Y.*

ception of Joseph Stella, he is the only American painter to have used cubism successfully for large-scale effect, while his expressionism belongs unmistakably to international trends. What I do mean is that Weber is a deeply professional artist in the European sense of the term, a man in whom the instinct for art is so dominant and unceasing that it absorbs all of him, constantly. He works independently of external reminder for the most part, and is relatively immune to the fluctuating promptings of season, hour and place to which men like Hopper and Burchfield have responded acutely. Weber's full identity is as an artist, and we feel in the best of his works a rapt intimacy with medium. He paints with a skill and purposefulness still infrequently found in American art. His art succeeds or fails, but it is always boldly signed; it has the maestro flourish, in the good meaning of the phrase.

Now consider Hopper. He studied at the Chase School of Art for five years under Robert Henri and Kenneth Hayes Miller. He went to Paris in 1906, remaining for a year, and he has returned there at intervals for holiday trips. In Paris he admired the works of the impressionists, but apparently heard nothing of the post-impressionists or of the brash leaders of new revolt, the *fauves*. He came home to witness and occasionally to take part in the brilliant series of exhibitions which announced American art's emancipation from nineteenth-century dominance: the Matisse show at Stieglitz's gallery; the one and only exhibition of "The Eight" at Macbeth's; the show organized by Robert Henri in a loft on 36th Street; the immortal Armory Show of 1913; the Forum exhibition of modern American painters at the Anderson Galleries (1916). But Hopper was not really one of the insurgents, and he mostly held apart from the furor, struggling instead against a personal discouragement which finally persuaded him to abandon painting for etching and commercial illustration during the years 1915–23.

To a certain degree Weber's reputation must stand or fall with what we self-consciously think of as "modern" art. But Hopper is a different matter. His case is the old one of the artist isolated from the prevailing tendencies of his time. It is the case of Ingres, for example, who let the regimentation of romanticism and realism pass him by, and was decried as a hopeless reactionary, though the most revolutionary artists of our own period have preferred him to Delacroix and Courbet. It is the case of Thomas Eakins who, to quote Hopper's words, "in the nineteenth century used the methods of the seventeenth, and is one of the few painters of the last generation to be accepted by contemporary thought in this country." Hopper's identification tag does not read "abstractionist" or "expressionist" or "surrealist," so that he is rejected by those who decide admission to posterity's levee on the basis of clamor outside the door. Yet Hopper belongs in essence to one of the strongest and most continuous of American pictorial traditions — realism. In the end, of course, only the factor of talent differentiates between the reactionary, academic artist and the artist temporarily appearing to be out of step. And if talent is a difficult point to decide on contemporaneously, it is one we may settle with some assurance in Hopper's case, after all these years of patient, steady accomplishment. His quality is his own, and he has made the most of it.

Max WEBER: Chassidic Dance, 1940. *Oil, 32 x 40". Collection Mr. and Mrs. Milton Lowenthal, New York.*

In 1908, when Weber returned to America, he brought with him four dominant impressions of his years of study in Europe. He remembered above all the sinuous Mannerism of El Greco, the solid masonry of Cézanne, the bold, sweeping arabesques of the *fauves,* the searing distortions of tribal sculpture. He remembered, too, at times, the Tuscan artists of the fourteenth and early fifteenth centuries, and turned occasionally to a primitivism which seems specifically Italian, as it often does in André Derain's paintings of 1909–13. In Weber's art of 1909–10, all these sources make themselves felt, sometimes in combination, sometimes alternately. By 1911, however, he seems to have recognized the need for a more cohesive approach. Perhaps at this stage of his career he was conscious that he must choose eventually between Matisse and Picasso, as Chassériau had had to choose between Delacroix and Ingres. Perhaps the issue was forced by the almost simultaneous appearance of Matisse's *La Joie de Vivre* and Picasso's *Les Demoi-selles d'Avignon*. If so, there can be no doubt that Picasso was to affect Weber the more profoundly, though as late as 1913 his old regard for Matisse flared up in his large panel, *Decoration with Cloud*. On the whole, however, he was headed away from *fauvisme* toward cubism. He was to arrive there by the same progression that Picasso himself had previously followed, with El Greco, Cézanne and African sculpture as guiding forces.

Between 1910 and 1912 Weber executed a number of small canvases in which the flowing volumes of the *fauve* style became jerky and sharp; the distortions of contour, whether Mannerist or African in derivation, became more and more geometric until they ended in a maze of cubist forms. It is possible to trace by stages in his work of this period the gradual formation of cubism's crystals, and a painting of 1912 is significantly entitled *Crystal Figures* — a logical sequence to the still-expressionist *The Geranium* of 1911 in which, Weber has declared, "The conception and treatment spring from a search of form in the crystal." But it is interesting to note how long the influence of primitive sculpture and of El Greco persisted within his cubist statement. Unlike Picasso, who appears to have left both Africa and Spain behind in one rush forward, Weber long retained a scholarly passion for tribal art, and he had found in El Greco a kindred figure in mysti-cism as well as esthetic aim. Even Weber's recent paintings of Jewish patriarchs (page 31) sometimes recall the twitching gesticulations of El Greco's saints, as though he ad-mired in Mannerism its religious longing no less than its asymmetric grace.

If Weber has been affected lastingly by the Spain which produced El Greco and Picasso, he has been affected, too, by the Russia where he was born and by the America to which he was brought as a child. His heritage as a Russian and a Jew has been most clearly recognizable since he abandoned cubism for a figure style of hieratic dignity, as in the numerous pictures of rabbis that he commenced to paint around 1918. Yet a child-hood memory of Russia and a strong racial inheritance may be felt even in certain of his cubist works. His cubism, unlike that of Picasso and Braque during the early years of the movement, was frequently almost exotic in color, and seemed to reflect the cacophonies of Russian folk art, the glitter of pageantry and the solemn richness of the synagogues. Furthermore, in such a work as the Museum of Modern Art's *Two Musicians* of 1917 (page 29), Weber's cubism includes a caricatural element which the Parisian cubists seldom employed and never, I think, to so pronounced a degree. Humanism is obviously an inescapable component of Weber's identity as an artist.

The impact of America on Weber's cubism was equally marked. To begin with, his painting shared with most cubist art produced in this country at the time of the First World War a use of Italian futurist devices to convey the special character of American subject matter. The Italian futurists, as I have indicated elsewhere in this book, longed for a brisk industrialism which existed in their country far less pointedly than in ours. The American cubists, on the other hand, were faced at first hand with a modern, urban mechanization, and inclined to use futurist forms to express it. Weber, for example, though his *Women and Tents* is presumably a Russian subject, soon began to depict through a cubist-futurist idiom various aspects of New York City, as in *Rush Hour, Chinese Restaurant* and other works of the First World War years. The spirit of these pictures is kaleidoscopic, and they depict panoramic, public scenes, in contrast to the Parisian cubists' devotion to single figures and still life. Together with Joseph Stella's fine paintings of Brooklyn Bridge, they constitute a most vigorous moment in modern American painting, a turning point, perhaps, in our country's attempt to draw abreast of advanced tendencies in European art.

At the end of the war Weber painted a second *Musicians* in which the figures emerge entirely from the cubist crystosphene. Until 1920 he reverted occasionally to a more abstract style, but after 1918 — his year of "introspection and discovery" as Alfred Barr calls it — he became primarily a painter of representational figures, still life and landscape, drawing occasionally on the archaic styles of the fourteenth century and earlier, as in his *Invocation* (1919). He now gave free rein to his pathos and humor, the one informed by a biting grandeur, the other remarkably acute, and he developed the expressionist figure style which may in the end prove to be his most substantial contribution to the art of our time.

For several years after the First World War Weber painted relatively few large-scale works. Then, in the mid-1920's, fluency returned to him, and the poignant intensity of his post-war canvases was relaxed in favor of a new painterly brilliance. His landscapes of the 1920's are sombrely romantic in their evocation of mood. Opposed to these are his still lifes in which a stress on sculptural form and on saturated color sometimes leads him uncomfortably close to Cézanne. Perhaps his finest pictures of the decade 1926–36 are the paintings of bathers in which he evolved those characteristic, stumpy nudes which seem like innocent sisters of Pascin's sturdy little prostitutes. The best of these figure pieces are skillfully defined; the line is restless, glowing and firm. Many of them — the *Eight Figures* of 1927, *At the Lake* of c. 1935 — are ambitious compositions, and the multiple figures are handsomely balanced through a rhythmic sweep of rounded forms. The color is rich and vibrant, and if Cézanne sometimes lurks in its shadows, its assurance is beyond the capacity of all but a few American artists. Mention must also be made of the small gouache sketches that Weber completed at this period. Some are absolute jewels, immense in carrying power, and compressing much of the purest artistic process within their diminutive scale.

Over the past ten years Weber has continued to paint with the acumen which has distinguished his career from the beginning. Possibly his most remarkable recent works have been those in which his early expressionism has been revitalized by the example of Picasso's *Guernica* and other works of the Spaniard's late career. This is not to say, of course, that Weber merely imitates Picasso; on the contrary, he is one of the few artists who has been able to convert the lessons of *Guernica* into a personal style. Consider, for example, the *Chassidic Dance* here reproduced (page 31). What magnificent action is conveyed by the whirlpool of feet and unflung claws! What compassionate satire in the faces and postures of the figures! The humor of the image exists on a very high level of creative invention. The picture itself summarizes Weber's character as an artist, illustrating his racial heritage, his monumentality, his control of Mannerist tensions, his wiry, deep line and brilliant color.

Quite apart from the intrinsic quality of Weber's painting, we in this country owe him much for providing a close and strong link between modern American art and the principal international trends of twentieth-century painting. He speaks a vernacular that may be understood everywhere by those who sympathize with the revolutionary visual achievements of our time. In doing this, he supplies an indispensable balance to those men who may one day find a world audience precisely because they now appear wholly American. Among these men is Edward Hopper.

I have already referred to the fact that, discouraged by painting, Hopper devoted himself to illustration and etching during the years 1915–23. There was nothing particularly startling or distinguished about his technique as an etcher, yet his prints were of the utmost importance for his career. To begin with, they sold well and were greatly admired, so that eventually Hopper was able to throw off his despair and return to watercolor and later to oil. Moreover, through etching he came to know what he had to say. His prints were not rendered from nature, but were composite inventions. They cleared his eye, so to speak, and when as a painter he returned to the use of actual models, he worked with a residual sense of selectivity, choosing and rearranging according to a settled and extremely personal vision. Several years ago, for example, he completed a painting, *August in the City,* which portrays one of the rounded, corner houses in the Riverside Drive section of New York. He had sketched the house in winter, but it emerged in his imagination as an image of summer, and he provided it with a wholly new *ambiance,* including a glade of trees which he is more likely to have seen on Cape Cod than in New York. The matter of his selectivity must be emphasized, for he is often dismissed as a simple realist, partly because he himself has followed Winslow Homer's precedent of utterly dispassionate self-analysis. "My aim in painting," he has said characteristically, "has always been the most exact transcription possible of my most intimate impressions of nature." But his "intimate impressions" have seldom been merely realistic. On the contrary, they have included a strain of lyric improvisation far more insistent than is generally recognized.

To return for a moment to his early etchings, it can be said that they furnish a remarkably complete index to the restricted compositional range he later adopted as a painter. His prints are nearly all horizontal or squarish in format, as his oils and watercolors have been since. Moreover, they include a majority of the structural patterns of his later art: the close-up horizontal band, unrelieved or broken by diminutive figures and objects; the broad, far horizontal panorama; the diagonal treatment of massive planes, as in his frequent three-quarter profile handling of architecture; the thrust of ascending curvilinear forms against rigid horizontal ones, evident in the etching, *Rail-*

Edward HOPPER: Gas, 1940. *Oil, 26¼ x 40¼″. The Museum of Modern Art, New York. Mrs. Simon Guggen-heim Fund.*

road, no less than in innumerable subsequent paintings; the predominantly horizontal mass interrupted by recessed parallel or oblique planes.

Since he began to paint again, Hopper has used all of these compositional formulas repeatedly, and this fact has naturally been cited as a serious limitation of his art. The truth is, however, that Hopper is one of those artists who, determined once and for all on a way of seeing, subordinate formal invention to intensity of realization. In the ulti-mate sense, he is as imaginative as some of our more aggressive contemporary fantasists. But like the Italian artist, Giorgio Morandi, he is absorbed in the expressive capacity of the commonplace and the familiar, and he would rather restate something revealingly than say something conspicuously new. "Anything will make a good composition," Hopper has said, and considering his gifts for intensification, he is perfectly right.

But how is this intensification managed? The color in Hopper's paintings is neither rich nor daring, though it has what Lloyd Goodrich has called "an unfatigued, hard vigor." The texture is usually uniformly rendered by smooth brushstrokes which leave no open trace of idiosyncratic touch; the drawing lacks flair entirely, and to devotees of

35

Tiepolo's bravura or Ingres' precision must seem not to be drawing at all. But what is almost always conveyed, what holds our attention in the best of Hopper's works, is the exceptionally clear and devout communication between the painter and his subjects. His language of seeming understatement has a backlash to it. It is not eloquent, but it is memorable, and his art has some of the dramatic force of evidence blurted in a courtroom, in an atmosphere of long circumlocution. He must be deeply stirred or he does not attempt to record his reaction. He works slowly, with infinite care, and sometimes goes through extended periods of inactivity between paintings. And perhaps the struggle his technique costs him accounts for the penetrating quality of his painting. For if the surfaces of his pictures are usually bland and unspectacular, their under-structure is exceptionally firm and sensitive. One has only to look at his recent handling of stone masonry to realize how sure his control of pigment can be. He gives New York's granite something of marble's inner illumination, and cuts its joinings with a sculptor's sense of form.

Most of Hopper's subjects have been found in New York, a city which offers the artist almost nothing of the pictorial order on which Parisian artists may so effortlessly feast their eyes. But Hopper walks the New York streets with an intent eye for evocative detail. He finds the warm gray stone, the Victorian bracket, the statue and the long borders of pavement, and these he describes with proud, frank love. His major expressive instrument, as many critics have noted, is light. He uses light variously, most often in bold chiaroscuro, but sometimes locally, as an almost invisible spray of highlighting. Light supplies the drama in most of his paintings, though typically it can be justified nearly always in the naturalistic terms of plausible source and reflecting surfaces. He is equally a master of the half-dark. Is there any living American painter able to suggest so well the huddled gloom of a grove of trees at evening?

If Hopper describes light with rare skill, he also records the density of air like the most delicate of barometers. A subtle gradation of atmospheric values is common to many of his finest works. In *Gas* (page 35), for example, the air seems to thin out as the eye moves from the bright area of the service station toward the thick woods across the road, light and the breeze waning together. The extremes of his atmospheric control are to be found in his depiction of absolute calm and the medium wind, and it is typical of his restraint that he should reject Homer's northeasters as too plainly dramatic. But he can bring the summer air to a dead halt — a far more difficult task than might be supposed — and he handles the wind with knowledgeable stagecraft. In this latter connection, one may fairly say that his etching, *Evening Wind* (1921), was prophetic of a recurrent preoccupation. The print shows a nude girl rising in bed to close the window against a storm which billows the draperies. In numerous paintings executed since that year, Hopper has used the flutter of curtains as a sign of heartbeat in the coma-like silence of his images.

When Hopper turns to pure landscape and to the seashore subjects which have occupied his summers these many years, he becomes with exceptions more nearly the unequivocal realist he has always professed to be, soaking his canvases in the brilliant

Edward HOPPER: Cornbelt City, 1947. *Oil, 20 x 36". The Frank K. M. Rehn Gallery, New York.*

American sunshine and giving the architecture of Cape Cod a look of rugged usability in which appear few traces of nostalgia for the past. Indeed he sometimes becomes rather dryly literal in his watercolors of the Cape, and his own special quality is obscured by an almost academic fussiness. But when he paints the city again, his sense of mood revives, and his window curtains divide two worlds of equal loneliness, indoors and out. His city and suburban houses are lonely; his streets are hushed and glum. He prefers the quiet hour and the lethargic season, as indicated by the titles of such pictures as *Sunday, Summer Time* and *Early Sunday Morning.* He shows the reverse side of the American industrial scene, with its gaudy energy and nervous pace; he reveals the sense of desertion and apathy often felt by a people which finds inadequate spiritual absorption in either recreation or work.

When the artist paints rooms rather than façades, a comparable lull in activity is usually evoked, and we may take his words on one of John Sloan's New York interiors as an indication that a romantic mood is consciously sought. Sloan's picture, Hopper declared, "renders remarkably the quality of a brooding and silent interior in this vast city of ours." Hopper's depiction of interiors is, however, more piercing in emotion than Sloan's and less often concerned with local color's cheerful familiarity. To give an extreme example, when Hopper paints the interior of a theatre, as in *Two on the Aisle,* he ignores the bustle and gay splendor which have attracted so many artists to this

37

subject. He shows the theatre empty save for three early arrivals, the curtain down for a quarter hour to come; he fixes the moments of self-conscious conversation and inattentive reading, and gives the sense of vacuity which comes from being alone in a place soon and inevitably to be thronged with people. Significantly, he is perhaps the only artist to have caught the special spirit of moving picture theatres — their dreamlike atmosphere, the intentness of the audience which escapes through the surrounding darkness to the flat, bright relief of the screen, projecting itself into the very forms of the drama, as in childhood shadow plays.

In many of Hopper's paintings the figures are reduced to an accessory role, and it must be admitted that he is a more skillful painter of architecture and landscape than of human beings, since he has never entirely thrown off a dependence on the rather lumpy figure style common to many graduates of the Chase-Henri school. Nevertheless, the pose of his figures is occasionally fresh and telling. His well-known *Hotel Lobby,* as one example, contains figures which symbolize acutely the gloomy pauses of travel. An elderly man and his wife fill the picture with their weariness, indecision and bleakness of mood. And in a corner sits the hard, muscular girl, sturdy of leg and breast, bulging her clothes, who reappears in many of Hopper's works — an obvious but somehow convincing Miss America, forthright in her sexual reality. Her clothes change only slightly from year to year, the length of her skirt hardly at all, and one will look in vain through Hopper's art for reflections of the drastic mutations of fashion which have taken place over the past twenty years. His world is fixed and timeless; its perennial ingenue is the helmeted post-flapper of the late 1920's and early 1930's.

Considered as a whole, Hopper's paintings furnish an extensive glossary of the human gestures of sadness and boredom — the figure sitting on a curbstone with huddled arms and staring eyes in *Sunday,* the woman in *Hotel Room* who holds unseeing a letter she has drained of all comfort, the girl in *Room in New York* who idly strikes a piano key while her husband reads the paper (Walter Sickert painted a similar subject and called it *Ennui,* but Hopper has fought clear of all but the most noncommittal titles). Yet it is for inanimate objects that Hopper reserves his most telling realism. By his handling of a window sill alone, he can indicate that a room is a dreary roost for humans, high above the pavement, brightly lighted, but cold, detached and confining.

Hopper is a subtle master of placing as well as of definition, and he often relocates elements of a given scene with cautious freedom, even after the over-all image has assumed more or less fixed form in his imagination. In this connection his words on Sloan again apply to himself. "Sloan," he wrote, "is one of those rarely fortunate artists who distorts unconsciously and to the point and without obvious process. His is the distortion that looks like truth and not that which looks like distortion." He added: "Sloan's design is the simple and unobtrusive tool of his visual reaction. It attempts tenaciously and ever the surprise and unbalance of nature, as did that of Degas. It composes by mass rather than perimeter and never attempts to shock by the bizarre."

The word "unbalance" in this quotation takes on particular meaning when we consider how often Hopper's own pictures are asymmetrically arranged, so that figures, lampposts and hydrants seem to have been included in his street scenes by accident rather than through plan. One sometimes feels, indeed, that these figures and objects have appeared unexpectedly within the artist's chosen vista, like shadows cast on a moving picture screen by figures crossing the projector's beam of light. Once they have appeared, Hopper records them faithfully, for they are signs of reality's wayward and unpredictable pattern, only slightly alterable in shape and place.

Hopper's mention of Degas in this connection is equally relevant, for it was the French master who founded in modern times the system of "unbalance and surprise" that later artists have adopted in varying degrees, substituting for the tactile standards of Baroque asymmetry a new basis of reference — the accidents of reality. Degas, of course, had developed the system under the influence of instantaneous photography and of Japanese prints, and such a Degas painting as the *Count Lepic and His Daughters,* with its informality of split-second pose, is the forerunner of a host of modern pictures in which compositional harmony is modified in favor of an emphasis on reality's chronic state of unbalance. But while Degas was absorbed in the shifting tensions of unposed figures and objects, Hopper's asymmetry is more phantomic in character. His people, lampposts and hydrants often occupy a marginal place rather than one of central and aggressive interest; the space around them is exaggeratedly open and bleak, to emphasize their fleeting and tenuous connection with a given locale.

There is, however, a danger in linking Hopper to so cultivated an artist as Degas. For while the Frenchman evolved his art from the great traditions of Italy and France, Hopper is by comparison a self-made painter working from a much narrower cultural heritage. Unlike Charles Demuth, he is not remarkable for the use he has made of divergent sources, but for his relative lack of sources. We cannot imagine Hopper producing the vast volume of work achieved by Degas and Renoir, inspired each day by art itself and never losing the urge for professional communication. Hopper is not a man for whom drawing or color is an unrelenting necessity. He works only when accumulated or sudden experience has inspired him with something to say. But his strength lies in the fact that he is so inartistic in the European sense of the term: no formalism, no seeking for graciousness, no painterly references; but self-invented realism, warm, convinced, romantic in overtone through its very bluntness of statement. If his expression cannot be compared in scope or power to that of leading Europeans, it is emphatically his own and American. Who abroad does what he does? Who there or here does it so well?

39

BEN SHAHN AND MORRIS GRAVES

There is a dwindling tendency among Europeans to think of American artists either as expatriate stylists or as homespun realists: West, Whistler and Sargent as guiding stars in one category; Eakins and Homer in the other. The distinction has been made most often in England, and quite naturally, for with the exception of Mary Cassatt all our most famous nineteenth-century exiles practised in London and contributed there to a worldly *ambiance* for art, West through academic position, Whistler through personal flamboyance, Sargent by social manipulation, their promotional methods changing with the nature of patronage. There can be no doubt that the talents of these artists were profoundly affected by their residence abroad, though we may still argue in what final degree. Today, however, the gains and penalties of expatriation are beside the point in considering the living artists of our two countries, for no first-rate American painter now centers his career anywhere but at home nor, I think, does any Englishman. Art has become so international in communication that it would be idle for a painter to live abroad merely to warm his wits; indeed, we may one day reach the stage where only the world capitals can harbor a limited provincialism within the insulating vigor of their own activity. Yet the actual genesis of painting and sculpture has perhaps become more national in very recent years, and it may be that we appreciate each other most when each speaks clearly his native language, instead of attempting a universal idiom.

A case in point is the favorable reception accorded two younger American artists at the Tate Gallery's 1946 exhibition of American painting. The artists are Ben Shahn (b. 1898) and Morris Graves (b. 1910). Both are decidedly American in identity; both are nourished by New World environment; and a fundamental difference between them is that Shahn looks outward for basic inspiration, while Graves looks inward.

Their childhoods were totally unlike. Shahn was born in Russia, came to America at the age of eight, and grew up in the poorer sections of Brooklyn. His art has never ceased to reflect the special atmosphere of life in an American metropolis. We cannot imagine him painting a landscape pure and simple, though urban architecture quite frequently supplies a dominant theme in his compositions, even if almost invariably accompanied by figures. He lives and works in the New Jersey countryside, for the sake of family comfort and freedom rather than through personal preference. He does not, however, live on a farm or in a picturesque village, as do so many American painters and writers. He lives at Roosevelt, New Jersey, in a Federal housing development for garment workers, built during the New Deal in the modern architectural style. He holds political office in his specialized community, and his first completed mural painting (1937–38) occupies a wall in the development's community center; its subject matter describes the betterment of his neighbors' lives through union membership. Shahn goes

Ben SHAHN: The Red Stairway, 1944. *Tempera, 18 x 24". City Art Museum, St. Louis.*

often to New York City, not only because he finds there the external properties which appear frequently in his works — factory buildings, tenements, lunchrooms, handball courts, and so on — but because there, most inescapably, the social issues of his time apply and are discussed. His unfailing nourishment is the reality of his period, though transformed by intensely imaginative gifts, as will appear.

Morris Graves is extremely different in personal temperament and in procedure as an artist. When he was a year old his family moved from Oregon to the Seattle area of the State of Washington, and except for travel in America and the Orient, he has lived there ever since, for several years now in a remote section of the seacoast near Anacortes, alone except for rare visitors, surrounded by the animals, rocks, pines and birds which are the subjects of his paintings. A deeply religious man, he has found the ideals of Vedanta sympathetic, but has held aloof from formal commitment to any cult. His existence consists largely in contemplation, and only after the most profound medita- tive preparation does he attempt to paint at all. To Shahn's tangible humanism, ex- pressed in his paintings and through frequent activity as a graphic-arts propagandist for

Government bureaus and labor organizations, Graves opposes a dissimilar yet morally related concept: the use of art as an instrument to deepen and clarify man's spiritual nature, to proceed, as he puts it, "toward the Eastern art's basis of considerations of metaphysical perceptions which produce creative painting as a record — an outflowing — of religious experience."

A safe generalization, then, would seem to be that Shahn is a realist and Graves a mystic poet, the one akin to Hogarth, the other to William Blake. Yet before settling on so final a differentiation between the two men, we must look more carefully at the factors affecting the development of each and at their art itself. Shahn, to begin with, was old enough when he left Russia to have absorbed the atmosphere of folklore and festival which characterized smaller Russian towns, so that in gaiety and richness of detail his mature painting sometimes parallels that of Marc Chagall. He was old enough, too, to have reacted to the oppressive social order in which his place was relatively fixed as the member of a humble Jewish family. As a child he developed a hatred of injustice — the only thing, he says, that he hates today. He has told in an interview of reading at school in Russia the story of the Ark of the Covenant's being brought to a temple and balanced precariously on a single pole, while God, as a test of faith, gave orders to the people that that no one should touch it, no matter what happened. "One man," Shahn recounts, "saw it beginning to totter, and he rushed up to help. He was struck dead. I refused to go to school for a week after we read that story. It seemed so damn unfair. And it still does." There could be no more revealing indication of Shahn's essential anti-mysticism of mind, his reverence for reality as opposed to myth, his belief in and conscience toward present circumstance.

Growing up in Brooklyn, Shahn found work as a lithographer's apprentice, like so many leading American artists of the nineteenth century and our own, and to this training may partly be attributed the precision with which he now handles lettering and intricate flowered patterns in certain of his pictures. He read a great deal, worked his way through several terms of college, and studied painting and sculpture at the National Academy of Design. In 1925 and again in 1927 he traveled widely in France, Italy, Spain and North Africa, and for several years thereafter painted in an expressionist manner which reflected his regard for Rouault and for those modern artists who had evolved a figure style of archaistic stylization based on pre-Christian, tribal and Mannerist sources. Then in 1930, he made up his mind that an art of esthetic sensation was alien to his temperament and heritage, that he was interested most of all in stories, people and social commentary. Between 1931 and 1934 he thereupon executed several series of small paintings, each series illustrating related incidents of a given theme, in the manner of Hogarth's *Marriage à la Mode*, except that the scenes did not follow a chronological sequence toward a moralizing climax, but were presented as more or less separable factual images. The two most extensive series were based on political *causes célèbres*, both American: the trial of the self-admitted anarchists, Sacco and Vanzetti, convicted in 1921, in the fury of a national "Red" hunt, for a murder they quite certainly

Ben SHAHN: Spring, 1947. *Tempera, 17 x 30″. The Downtown Gallery, New York.*

did not commit (they were executed in 1927) ; and the case of the persecuted labor leader, Tom Mooney. The two series won Shahn a considerable fame and the esteem of the Mexican muralist, Diego Rivera, whose assistant he became for a short time, and whose ideological and technical influence on the younger painter is apparent in Shahn's first mural at Roosevelt, New Jersey.

Graves' beginnings were decidedly different. He grew up in the superbly wild landscape of the Washington coast. He completed his secondary education, but with the exception of brief training under a high school art instructor, he learned to paint mainly by experiment and by association with artists he admired. In 1930 he worked his way to Japan. This and a subsequent voyage to the Virgin Islands (1940) have been of great importance in his development. His rapt memories of the East have been reinforced in more recent years by a close study of the fine Oriental collections in American museums, notably the Seattle Art Museum, and by an appreciation of the researches of such art historians as Dr. Ernest Fenollosa and Dr. Ananda Coomaraswamy. Gradually his interest in the Orient has focused almost exclusively on Japan, most urgently on Kyoto where he hopes one day to explore the art collections in museums, monasteries and private homes. He is passionately interested in the architecture of Japan as well, and in its celebrated gardens and its crafts.

If Graves has turned to the Orient for inspiration, he is also aware of twentieth-

43

century developments in European and American art, and some years ago was greatly influenced by them. He speaks with respect of Chagall — I do not know what attracts him to so disparate an artist. He is often and much too glibly compared to Paul Klee. He knows and admires Klee's art, but it is a curious paradox that his regard for the late German master is mild in relation to that of Shahn, the realist, who worships Klee's paintings and has consciously emulated some of their virtues, as we shall see. And on the whole Graves and Klee are immeasurably separate. Klee was a painter of such varied imaginative endowment that everything he touched took on a special identity, changing from picture to picture. A wine glass could inspire him as well as a flower, and through much of his art there ran a tremendously alert humor which cut to the heart of profundity. Graves, on the other hand, is by comparison single-minded and single-visioned, and we nearly always feel in him the sway of a continuous, dark mood, not lacking in humor, but too brooding for wit. This, of course, is his strength, as Klee's faceted sensitivity was his. And in his absorption in nature, Graves may more rewardingly be compared to another modern American artist, Charles Burchfield, whose early watercolors, as I have said, are among the high points of native romantic art. But there is this difference to be noted: while Burchfield recorded the preternaturalism imagined by a susceptible child, Graves lets nature's tensions play out all within nature itself — the bird against the forest silence, the giddy snake against the moon.

The 1930's were difficult years for Graves. During the mid-decade depression years, he and friends wandered through the West in a car, painting, and attempting to sell their pictures by the roadside. In 1937 he came to New York City. Unlike Shahn, for whom New York has provided a constant stimulus, Graves was confused and disturbed by the city, and at one point sought refuge with Father Divine in Harlem, supporting himself by doing menial tasks for "angels" of the cult. He was indifferent to New York's architecture and, typically, the scene which moved him most was that of a pigeon dying in the street; he bent over the bird and made a series of devout sketches. He returned to Seattle in 1938, and began to paint in oil and encaustic, modeling a heavy impasto to almost sculptural depth. He was employed at this time by the Federal Government's W.P.A. art project, and it is to the everlasting credit of that project that it should have supported a "private" artist like Graves as well as a "public" artist like Shahn. Some of Graves' works of this period were planned in series, like Shahn's, and some, too, were related to external events — the "Purification" series to the death of Pope Pius XI, the superb series of drawings, "English, French, German and Roman Nightfall," to the Munich Pact. But in none of these pictures is there any reference to specific happening; all are symbolic equivalents for inner yearning and despair. The "Purification" series consists of a group of abstract variants on landscape sections, many with chalices monumentally enthroned, as if these were models of the Anacortes hills laid out with Japanese delicacy of asymmetric perception. The "Nightfall" series portrays a suite of ruined and animated furniture suitable for a meeting of a "Gothick" or surrealist conclave. The chairs are strung over with precise red cobwebs, and no one sits in them, though the

Morris GRAVES: Bird Singing in the Moonlight, 1938–39. *Gouache, 26¾ x 30⅛". The Museum of Modern Art, New York.*

faces of Hitler, Chamberlain and Daladier would have proved irresistible to Shahn, had he undertaken the theme. Yet the spirit of Graves' "Nightfall" drawings is strangely urbane; their bizarrerie has something of the knowledgeable precision of a Callot or a Fuseli; they are sophisticated drawings even if one senses in them a lonely strength.

Toward the end of 1938 Graves adopted the technique by which we know him today — gouache and watercolor applied on thin, wavery Chinese paper or on *Kakemono* scrolls. His change in direction was not merely technical, however. On his return to Seattle he had come under the influence of Mark Tobey, an older artist of remarkable sensitivity who, after long experiment with advanced expressive means, had evolved what he called an art of "white writing" — a psychic scribble which ran over the picture surface and conveyed a cat's-cradle image of the painter's response to outer experience and religious compulsion. Tobey had adopted the technique around 1935, after a trip to the Orient during which he had studied with the Chinese artist, Teng Kwei, but very likely his interest in the tenets of Bahai had been a more decisive influence. Graves, too, in the late 1930's was turning away from a material chaos toward a contemplative anagoge, and Tobey's painting struck him with tremendous force. Within a short time he had abandoned the thick impasto of his earlier pictures, and had adapted Tobey's "white writing" to his own spiritual needs, developing its gouache and watercolor technique in a manner wholly his own. He now used a semi-automatic calligraphy to create a supernatural and romantic vision of the birds, snakes and small animals which fought each other and obeyed the moon on the rocky Anacortes coast. I say "semi-automatic," for however spontaneously Graves' imagery may seem to evolve from his imagination, in final form it is often the result of long deliberation and careful revisions.

But meanwhile Shahn. After completing the Sacco-Vanzetti and Mooney series, he spent a good part of the succeeding ten years (1933–43) on public projects, as the employee of Federal agencies. While working on the Government's Public Works of Art Project, he completed a series of tempera paintings on Prohibition (1933–34). These were followed by designs for murals showing old and reformed penal methods, commissioned as a Federal Emergency Relief Administration project. The murals themselves were intended for a prison corridor at Riker's Island near New York City, but were never executed because of academic opposition, though a poll of prisoners proved an overwhelmingly favorable reaction to the sketches. In 1937–38 Shahn finished for the Farm Security Administration the single-wall mural at Roosevelt, New Jersey, previously mentioned. With the help of his wife, he next completed a far more ambitious project for the U.S. Treasury's Public Buildings Administration: a series of fresco panels covering the walls of the Bronx post office and comprising a panorama of American industry and agriculture. The same Federal agency commissioned him to paint murals for the Social Security Building in Washington, D.C.; these illustrate the benefits of Social Security for the old, the poor, the dispossessed, and were completed between 1940 and 1942. During the war Shahn designed several brilliant posters for the Office of War Information, and from 1944 to 1946 was director of the graphic arts division of a left-wing labor organization.

In devoting so much of his time to communal projects, in taking sides aggressively on social issues, Shahn would seem to be the absolute opposite of Graves, whose pictures do not exhort the observer but rather hold a finger to his lips. Thus, on the basis of art's intended use, we arrive again at our early differentiation: Shahn the realist; Graves the mystic poet. We shall be mistaken if we accept the opposition as total. For quite apart from his public projects, Shahn has worked fairly steadily as an easel painter, and has developed over the past ten years into one of the most lyric of living American painters as well as into one of our most original satirists. If reality gives him a point of departure that he will never willingly lose from sight, he nevertheless transforms his

46

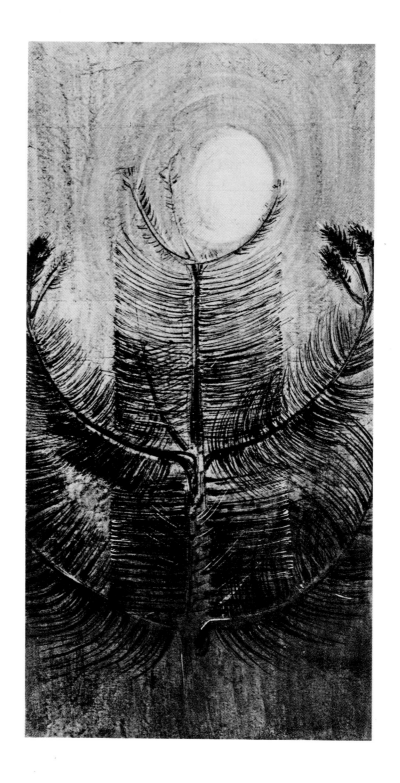

Morris GRAVES: Joyous Young Pine, 1944. *Watercolor and gouache,*
535/8 x 27". The Museum of Modern Art, New York.

images through the most subtle and poetic intervention of his pictorial imagination. I have spoken of his great esteem for Klee. In his own paintings the drawing often has a witching, autonomous energy comparable to Klee's — "a red line on white paper has a nervous identity of its own," as Shahn puts the matter. His structure does not evolve from realistic observation merely, but makes full use of the intensifying deformations to be found in cubism and its later, abstract ramifications. His color is frequently as arbitrary as that of the French symbolists or the German expressionists, and departs from probability whenever he wishes to stress or enliven a moral, emotive or plastic content. A gifted photographer, he has used photographs as other artists use rough sketches, and was once greatly disturbed because for a time he could not find a building which appeared in one of his pictures, though he was sure he had seen it somewhere. Yet however strong his mistrust of fantasy-for-its-own-sake, he revivifies reality according to subjective expressive needs. No one, for example, can look at *Spring,* here reproduced (page 43), without being aware that Shahn is the heir to modern visual trends as well as of an earlier naturalism.

In late years Shahn has gradually tended to lessen the satirical impact of his easel painting, moving toward an elegiac art more closely related to European traditions than ever before (page 41). His first mature works — the Sacco-Vanzetti and Mooney series — had stressed the effect on the individual of organized and oppressive social forces. Toward the end of the 1930's, he began to portray the individual in terms of private emotional experience, and from this period dates a group of pictures conceived on Sunday excursions through the New Jersey countryside, pictures of American loneliness, of the single figure dwarfed by space, the idle man in a listless void. At the same time, he painted many images of children at play, depicting their appearance and gestures with magic acuteness, and suggesting unforgettably their imaginative seizures. The recent war inspired him to paint, as a kind of lyric mourning, a group of pictures in which he dwelt most often on Italy's ruined architecture, the sad lethargy of the homeless relieved by the fantasy of children playing amid the slithered, immortal stones. Since the war Shahn has alternated European with American subjects; his pictorial freshness, his conviction, his technical mastery have become steadily more impressive. We might sometimes call him now a gracious artist, spiritual ally of the fourteenth-century Sienese, Fra Angelico, the brothers Le Nain, where once he seemed to belong wholly to the harder, satirical tradition. But reality is still his talisman, as it was for Théodore Géricault, and he is still concerned with public benefit from his art. Several of his recent paintings have been made into political or humanitarian posters by the addition of lettering, and perhaps no other living American artist, nor any of the past, has so successfully combined propaganda with esthetics, not alternating one with the other, but fusing the two with rare integrity.

Just as Shahn cannot be described simply as a realist, so Graves is not as detached a mystic as is sometimes supposed. His finished gouaches are so poetically transformed that we do not always realize how rich a treasury of nature's forms his memory holds.

Indeed, the best of his works have an uncanny sense of privacy, as though they had not been witnessed by the painter, but had been recorded on enchanted film by shutters tripped in the primeval dark, with no one near. Nevertheless, many of his paintings partly depend for effect on an underlying sense of reality, incalculably attained, as when he portrays sandpipers, gulls or mice with emphasis on some mannerism of action or pose that establishes character as well as identity. Of course, even when he comes this near to realism, his images are weighted toward symbolism by an atmospheric use of "white writing," and by the abstracting process of his design. He shifts the balance between the "actual" and the "imaginary" with great variety of intention and result. In some of his pictures and in many of his drawings, the actual plays a vigorous role — his sandpipers shoo a wave across the sand, a mouse congeals with fear. But in other paintings he achieves an art of nocturnal signs and omens: an owl is wrapped in a quilt of dreams; a snake rears hysterically at the moon; a blind bird ponders its hallucinations. His is an observation which learns particulars by heart in order to express a supernal generality. He is perhaps most successful when he utilizes both his inner and outer eye. In the *Bird Singing in the Moonlight* (page 45), the cloud of moonlight which envelops the bird in chalice form is ectoplasmic in feeling. But the bird's beak and cumbersome legs are sharply real. Similarly, the tender humor of the drawing in this picture plays against the abstract texture of the color — factual recognition and legerdemain existing together in an evocative synthesis.

I began by saying that Shahn and Graves were decidedly American as artists, and so they are. However important Shahn's Russian heritage may be, however near he draws at times to foreign lyricism, we cannot conceive of his art's being produced elsewhere than in the American environment. This is not a matter of subject matter alone, but of the pulse and nerves of his paintings, evident in his recent idyllicism no less than in his early satire, and epitomized somehow in the description of his art that Shahn likes best — "hardboiled — and beautiful." And Graves, though his philosophical approach to art is based on Oriental example, worships the landscape of our Northwest (page 47), and in his pictures may be felt the same wild heartbeat which distinguishes Audubon's images from those produced contemporaneously in older countries. Like our great modern architect, Frank Lloyd Wright, Graves has transfused Japanese spiritual principles to an American empiricism; he has not merely applied a descriptive flair to exotic subjects, as did John La Farge and other earlier American painters who loved the Orient.

Shahn and Graves belong, respectively and in essence, to two of the oldest and most continuous American traditions in art: the realism which produced Copley, Eakins and Homer; and the romanticism which claimed Washington Allston, the Hudson River School, Albert Pinkham Ryder and Robert Newman. These two traditions, however, have touched hands often during their march, and few of our painters since the early nineteenth century have belonged to one or the other so whole-mindedly as Eakins and Ryder, our most unequivocal realist and our greatest romantic. As I have suggested in these pages, Shahn has sometimes abstracted his visual experience with such tenderness that the word "romantic" seems appropriate to him in a limited sense, while Graves, for all his reliance on supernatural awareness, can tell us the exact weight of a plover's wing.

Both artists supply convincing evidence that neither of our two great pictorial traditions is anywhere near spent, though the self-conscious modernists, who hold that all art begins with Cézanne and Picasso, would have us think otherwise. Finally, what is especially heartening about Shahn and Graves, from the American viewpoint anyway, is that they, among others, clearly obviate the old distinction between the knowledgeable expatriate and the provincial homebody. Living and working in this country, they have taken what they needed from foreign sources, Shahn from Europe, Graves from the Orient. For American painters, situated as they are, it should be as natural to look East or West as for French artists to look north to Flanders and England or south to Greece and Italy. The careers of Shahn and Graves prove, I think, that our painters are at last able to look either way without losing the indigenous sense of direction without which art is merely a vacuous wind careening over a dead sea.

PETER BLUME

In July, 1937, Peter Blume finished *The Eternal City,* a medium-sized painting on which he had worked without interruption since October, 1934. The picture, together with related drawings, was exhibited in New York soon after completion, and provoked a divided but largely vituperative reaction among critics. The main charge against the artist was that he had abandoned the contemporary idiom of his earlier works for a return to allegory and the technical methods of the fifteenth century. In the final analysis, however, contemporary expression is only what is said with authority contemporaneously, as the history of art repeatedly proves, and Blume's picture gains stature each year as one of the most remarkable paintings produced by a living American artist, regardless of age. This, admittedly, is personal opinion, yet *The Eternal City* is admired today by many more serious critics than it was when it was completed. Perhaps we believe less firmly now in progress as something self-contained and peculiar to our times; perhaps we are less self-conscious in our modernity, less certain that we know in what it consists. At any rate, we are beginning to admit again the validity of earlier contentions: that the artist can profess as well as confess; that the painter may derive his material from moral ideas no less than from hedonistic sensations; that art is not measure only, nor release nor pleasure, but may also be a sign and a tract.

What has Blume produced since *The Eternal City?* Part of that painting's distinction was that it represented a concentrated effort extremely rare in American art. When it was finished, the artist quite naturally experienced an exhaustion that was deepened by the reception accorded his picture. He overcame his depression in a painter's way, by painting a new work — the *Lilies,* now in the Boston Museum. The picture is as carefully executed as anything he has done, but is almost therapeutically restricted in theme. It portrays a simple arrangement of flowers on the window sill of Blume's studio at Gaylordsville, Connecticut. No trace remains of the tremendous ideology of *The Eternal City;* the color is muted and pale; the forms are nearly as abstract as in some of his very first canvases, in which the influence of Le Corbusier's and Ozenfant's purism and of the American "Immaculates" — Sheeler, Demuth, Preston Dickinson — may be felt. One surmises that in *Lilies* Blume rested his imagination and chastened his eye, though he arrived nonetheless at a handsome work of art.

In 1938 Blume was commissioned by Edgar J. Kaufmann to paint a picture of and for his famous Frank Lloyd Wright house at Bear Run, Pennsylvania. The commission was ill-fated, and from it evolved only a few fine drawings and a small painting of this brilliant house. Perhaps one reason for this was that Blume, who had handled mechanical architectural forms masterfully in *Parade, South of Scranton,* and *Light of the World,* had become engrossed in an animistic conception of nature. Whereas previously he had emphasized a static balance of inanimate objects, he now was drawn to the wayward and curious forms of stones, twigs, flowers and roots. The interest was first announced by *Landscape with Poppies,* painted in 1939. The picture shows no particular eccentricity of motif, but in it the painter takes up a rapt stance before nature, using an intimate perspective, as if the scene were viewed by a child lying on the ground and staring at a diminutive landscape all within reach.

Blume spent the winter of 1940 at Key West, Florida. There, on the tropical beaches, he found a strange, cacophonous array of rusted stones and gleaming coral, seaweed like wild hair, buoys and rotting chains, all the inexplicable jetsam of the sea. He returned home to paint a series of small oils and to execute numerous pencil drawings of the material he had found. *Buoy* (opposite), *Key West Beach* and *Weathervane* are aggressive manifestations of an imaginative fantasy that Blume had held under more conscious control in earlier works. The color in these pictures is bright and forceful, their textural manipulation more pronounced than ever before. But what gives them their ultimate distinction is their psychological impact, their obsessive vigor as images derived from the farthest recesses of the artist's subconscious mind. None of them assumes a specific human configuration, but all stir with an allusive force which in *Weathervane* becomes frankly sexual in connotation.

At this time Blume produced in related vein a number of automatic drawings which he called by the familiar term "doodles," though many were highly finished in technique. Their number increased until very recently, and they now constitute an exceptional document on one of the most fertile imaginations in modern American art. For there is this paradox to be noted in Blume's career. He is one of the most painstaking craftsmen now painting in this country; he has devoted his twenty-odd years as an artist to less than fifty pictures, several of them climactic works involving long preparation and summarizing a slowly accumulated fund of imagery. One would say, then, that he is the very type of formal artist, saving himself for concentrated efforts and depending for impetus on the most intensive premeditation. But his is also a temperament of sudden gusts, sensitive to fugitive impressions which he records mainly in his "doodles," but also sometimes includes in major compositions. His process of final selection is customarily slow, yet the material from which he selects is vivid and quick; he is always open to chimerical suggestion. Classic in his ultimate restraint, he is romantic in his acceptance of the apparitions which appear in the more obscure regions of his alert, nervous mind.

It is another paradox of Blume's career that he has often spent months on a small canvas, while his three mural commissions for the U.S. Treasury's Public Buildings Administration were completed each in a matter of weeks. All three murals measure seven by fourteen feet; all were painted in oil at his Gaylordsville studio and later mounted on the walls for which they were intended. The first, entitled *Beatty's Barns,* was completed in 1937 and installed in the post office at Cannonsburg, Pennsylvania; it shows the farm buildings of a neighbor in the Housatonic Valley, which Blume knows by heart. The second, *Vineyard* (1941), in the post office at Geneva, New York, is a

Peter BLUME: Buoy, 1941. *Oil, 18 x 20". Collection Dr. Flanders Dunbar, Key West.*

relatively free improvisation, and portrays a monstrous grapevine projected against a far river landscape, its bulging contours related to Piero di Cosimo's grotesque naturalism. The third mural is entitled *Two Rivers* (1943), and is mounted in the court house and post office building at Rome, Georgia; its subject is a composite image of the town where it hangs, with one river coming down clear from the hills and another emerging red from the clay fields through which it has passed.

Blume clearly thought of all three murals as decorative works in which the intensity of his easel art was not required. Yet all are carefully planned and carried out, and they make clear that it is not the problem of execution which primarily accounts for Blume's slow production; he has produced few easel paintings because in each he has tried to transcend decorative requirements and to achieve through constant experiment and ruthless introspection the most positive statement of perseverant ideas of which he is capable.

In 1944 Blume was commissioned as a civilian to prepare a painting of a self-chosen subject at the Army's Halloran General Hospital, Staten Island, New York. He sketched in the hospital for several weeks, and months later produced an oil painting, *Penicillin Ward, Army Hospital,* now in the possession of the U.S. Army's Medical Department. The composition is notable for its skillful and subtle use of complementary images within the over-all scene: in the foreground two figures with arm injuries are studying a map of the war in which they were casualties; a wounded man in bed works at therapy on a "waffle rug" whose crisscross structure repeats, small scale, the elaborate framework above the beds which supports the weights of the traction splints. Blume himself once remarked: "I like the references of pictures within pictures." *Penicillin Ward* is especially rich in such references. Moreover, the handling of the perspective in the tiled floor and the scaffolding is unusually sure, the wounded Negro in the background a remarkable figure. Both as humanist document and as painterly treatise, the picture is one of the most notable American paintings relating to the recent war.

In 1945 Blume began work on his fifth major composition, the previous four being *Parade* (1930), *South of Scranton* (1931), *Light of the World* (1932) and *The Eternal City* (1934–37). The new picture is tentatively entitled *Excavation,* and in preparation for it the artist has produced a small painting by the same name which shows a section of the large composition (opposite), now considerably altered. He has also completed a series of fine preliminary drawings of figures, in which the meticulous technique of his earlier figure-pieces is replaced by a new and bold treatment of sweeping action. These drawings relate to the figures in the painting itself, but it is an interesting fact that Blume does not refer to them in working on the big canvas. "Their chief value," he says of the drawings, "lies even more in the experience of having done them than in the ideas and movements which they suggest."

The theme of the new picture is man's struggle with the under-earth. It is a violent and bitter struggle. Nature fights the intrusion on her subterranean privacy; her wild and broken roots gesticulate toward immaculate masonry walls; her stones grate heavily on the laborer's shovel. The animism announced by the Key West series is here developed with extraordinary variety and originality. In the center of the picture rests a fantastic melon-like form, huge in its suggestion of scale, magnificent in richness of color and texture. The form rests on a sort of mesa, on which appear strange fragments of fungus and clay that writhe and twist like protagonists of a supernatural drama. At the base of this central structure, workers shift slabs of marble or dig into the earth, their eloquent distortions related, however indirectly, to those of the figures in *Penicillin Ward*. At the right of the composition a half-ruined factory rises to the sky; at the left appears the

Peter BLUME: Excavation, 1945. *Oil, 21 x 27". Owned by the artist.*

terraced building under construction toward which all this labor with the earth is directed. A sense of tremendous drama is conveyed, not only by the picture as a whole, but by various details which never dominate the over-all image but add to its intensity and liveliness. In the right foreground, for example, some scattered stones are painted with such luminosity and grandeur of spacing that they seem a world in themselves, like the stones of Bellini or Patinir.

This picture, even in its present unfinished state, is answer indeed to those who accused Blume of retrogression when he abandoned the abstract fantasies of his earlier career for the ambitious polemic of *The Eternal City*. He has not gone backward at all. On the contrary, he has gone forward with a strength and conviction that single him out as one of the major American painters of our century, one of the few who understand and accept fully the demands of the true creative process.

LOREN MacIVER

Of facts relating to the career of Loren MacIver, none seems more pertinent than that she received all her brief training in art as a child of ten, at the Art Students League. Since that early age, she has developed into one of the most knowledgeable of living American painters, a slow, skilled, eloquent master of craft. But it was as a child that she first wanted to be an artist, and her painting has never lost the intensity of childhood longing for expression and communication. Even in youth, MacIver's aptitude for discovery and concentration must have been unusual. I imagine she was the child who stayed behind and stared at a blossom or a stone, while her companions scattered in changing, forgetful excitement.

MacIver grew up in New York City, where she was born in 1909, and though she loves and has painted the country too, hers is instinctively an art of the city. Today, when nature appears in her pictures, it appears usually as a captive. Her flowers bloom defiantly on a push cart, or lie spent on a garbage heap; her trees sprout stars behind a Victorian fence in spring; her pears and grapes are curios displayed at a downtown corner stand. But nature, brought captive from afar, takes on a special radiance in the city, and Mac-Iver runs close to her in the street and lifts her veil.

For the most part she now paints what is peculiarly the city's own — the blister of summer pavements, the tremble of votive lights, the deliberate spread of an oil slick on the impatient river, the chalk marks left by children to describe their games, their passions, their wounds and threats. Hers is an art of magic awareness, discovery after discovery: a shy, tiptoe art through which she recaptures childhood's ecstatic peering. Mac-Iver makes us look for what she herself customarily sees, a sure sign of the artist, and I for one can never walk through Central Park without noticing images she might have painted. Yet we cannot easily predict what will catch her attention, and when we think we know the limits of her response, she opens new corridors, quietly.

MacIver only occasionally uses metaphor in describing what she sees, but she has her own ways of rarifying observation: by atmospheric enclosure; by an abstract rearrangement of forms; by use of color as a sorcerer's dust, settling lightly. She alternates between the panorama and the close-up. In such works as *The City* (1941) and *The Violet Hour* (1943), she has created pictographs of New York, with abundant, packed detail. But then again, to borrow a term from photography's lexicon, she changes the lens of her vision from wide-angle to telephoto, and portrays the fragment large-scale, squinting with alert eyes at small phenomena that normal sight would scarcely heed.

Of course MacIver has learned certain lessons from her contemporaries. Perhaps of these Klee has meant most to her, for it was assuredly he who founded the particular art of lyric recognition which she has followed. But she sees with her own inquisitiveness,

56

Loren MacIver: Red Votive Lights, (1943). *Oil on wood, 20 x 25⅝". The Museum of Modern Art, N.Y.*

and with a reticence that is deft rather than afraid, so that naturally Emily Dickinson's femininity and wonder come to mind. At times — I think especially of a picture called *Moonlight* — Picasso has influenced her, though she strips his later art of savagery, and retains for her own purposes only its fitful, hieroglyphic brilliance. Among modern American artists she most admires John Marin, quite probably for his spontaneity, yet her own painting seems closer, in its quiet mysticism, to that of the late Arthur Dove.

"My wish," MacIver has said, "is to make something permanent out of the transitory, by means at once dramatic and colloquial." Her colloquialism is apparent in her choice of humble subjects, and for the grand sentiments of history-painting she substitutes brief lyrics in praise of the "unimportant," the discarded, the mute. What is difficult to explain, however, is the process through which she dramatizes the commonplace.

Perhaps we may begin by saying that her control of illumination is exceptionally fine. Her lighting has little to do with realistic source or with chiaroscuro as a modeling device. Instead, her objects are lighted according to the nature and degree of her subjective reaction. The theme of many of her pictures is incandescence, the warmth which arises in her imagination when she comes on scenes or objects that move her profoundly. She likes the uneasy light of candles, the bright surfaces of Christmas ornaments, glittering even in the half-dark. She has made a series of pictures of votive lights (page 57), in various over-all tonalities — "flickering and vanishing, become symbols of constancy," she says. She uses light as an emotional diagnostic, moving it about like the miniature flashlight of physicians. It is often her control of incandescence that gives her images their curious vitality, as when she converts the contents of an ashcan into a ritual offering by bathing them in a sacramental light.

MacIver handles texture with equally remarkable sensitivity, and is essentially a painter of surfaces. In the Museum of Modern Art's *Hopscotch,* perhaps her best known picture, a section of cracked, bubbled pavement is defined by built-up impasto, while on an adjoining, bland section appear the scuffled figures of a hopscotch court. Her painting is often a record of those endlessly varied marks whereby human character is stamped on objects of use. I remember, for example, a recent picture of a duck decoy in which subtle modulations of color suggest handling and wear, with rare poignancy. MacIver customarily prefers what man has touched. There is a significant contrast of spirit between her wooden decoy and one of Morris Graves's wild, unapproachable birds.

MacIver's best pictures are executed in the soft, smoky colors she has made so completely her own. In her sensitivity to the oil medium's capacity for expressing a shy sensuality, she seems related to Pierre Bonnard, though both her technique and her palette are entirely different. A nearer counterpart in use of color, among artists who have had no influence on her whatever, would be the late Gwen John in England. It can be no accident that these two women have painted with a comparable intuitive freshness, however unlike their pictures are. One reason for the extension of art's perceptive range in recent times may be that women have made so special a contribution. Indeed, before we are through with our century's visual accomplishment, we may discover that it has been vivified by women in some such degree as was the novel long ago, by Jane Austen, the Brontës, and others.

Finally, MacIver is one of our finest portraitists, at her best with children and with a few public figures who have for her a most private meaning. As might be expected, she is acutely aware of the inner personalities of the young. But her outstanding portraits to date are those of two clowns whose talents she reveres: Jimmy Savo, a close personal friend; and Emmett Kelly, star of the Ringling Brothers' circus. Of Savo she has painted a three-quarter length picture which captures his fey gentleness of pose and gesture, his slyness, poignancy and piercing expressive means. In this picture the emphasis is on Savo's hands, which gesticulate wryly, like the arms of carefully controlled puppets. When MacIver paints Emmett Kelly, on the other hand, her approach changes entirely. For this great clown's quality springs from stillness rather than animation: he stands alone in the vast circus tent, and holds his audience by his solemnity, and enormous,

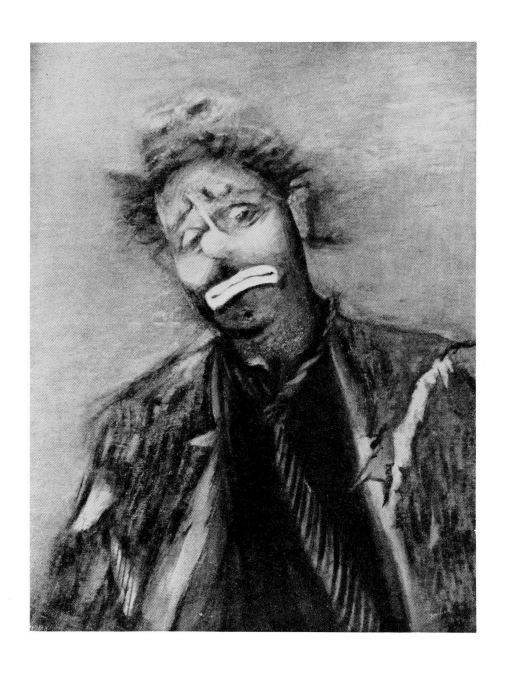

Loren MacIver: Emmett Kelly, 1947. *Oil. 40 x 32". Collection Mr. and Mrs. Roy R.*
Neuberger, New York.

shadowy dignity. MacIver has painted a pastel head of Kelly, showing the sad, hypnotic face in traditional clown's make-up — wide, white mouth and bulbous nose. Perhaps her most impressive portrait to date, however, is the half-length oil of Kelly here reproduced (page 59). The image looms forward from its atmospheric background, tentative yet insistent, reticent yet strong. This kind of almost phantomic portraiture is seldom found in American art, though precedent is furnished by Washington Allston's romantic portraits of William Ellery Channing and Benjamin West, completed early in the nineteenth century. But how daring is the fading, smudged area of the hat in MacIver's picture, and how well it holds our attention despite the aggressive white lips of the clown! Warm, tender, intensely alive, the image deserves an important place in modern American figure painting.

If our country now has painters of greater vigor than MacIver, it has none, I think, whose art is more evocatively refined or surely expressed.

MATTA ECHAURREN

An event of decided interest in the recent New York art scene has been the emergence of Roberto Sebastian Antonio Matta Echaurren as the latest, perhaps for a time the last, important painter of the surrealist movement. Matta was born in Santiago, Chile, in 1912, of Spanish lineage. He once related an anecdote, based on a poem by García Lorca, to explain what a Spanish heritage could mean to an artist. A thief in Barcelona, he said, dressed in his finest clothes and went along the quays stealing lemons. When he had gathered as many as he could carry, he walked to the river, threw the lemons in, and watched them float away. Apprehended and brought to court, he explained: "I have never seen the river so black or such bright yellow lemons." Thereupon the judge escorted him to the door and freedom, a carriage of justice not likely to have occurred elsewhere than in Catalan Spain, as Matta pointed out.

Matta's own yellows often float in black pools of pigment, but though he prefers to think of himself as Spanish, his first paintings were notable for a Latin-American exuberance of color — tropical yellows, blues, reds and greens running over the canvas like thin lava. He came to this country in 1939 from Paris, where he had studied architecture in Le Corbusier's office, his family having insisted that he become an architect rather than a painter. He was enrolled in Le Corbusier's office for three years, but apparently worked there only a few months out of the year, and spent the remainder of his time traveling or conversing with the Parisian surrealists whose group he joined officially in 1937.

During his apprenticeship as an architect, Matta stayed for some time in England. Did he admire there the late paintings of Turner, in which form dissolves in a spreading flame of color? He speaks casually of Turner's art, with no marked respect, yet among paintings of modern times Turner's are perhaps nearest in spirit to his own early works, with two important exceptions — Kandïnsky's free improvisations of 1911–18 and Miro's untypical but altogether impressive painting of 1937, *Still Life with Old Shoe*. As to Matta's connection with earlier sources, his veiled hills, jets of fire and rolling fogs are related, however distantly, to the sixteenth-century nocturnal mysticism exemplified by such separate works as Grünewald's "Temptation of St. Anthony" panel at Colmar and Beccafumi's "Victory of St. Michael" at Siena. Significantly, his tissues of flaming color have often assumed the Mannerist forms of El Greco, notably in a canvas of 1942, *The Disasters of Mysticism*.

Whatever Matta's affinity to previous artists, he has reinvented in personal terms the use of fluidity as a vehicle for semi-automatic expression. His painting has changed drastically over the past few years, as will appear, but we may wonder whether he was once in some degree a prophet as well as an artist. At least his pictures of 1939–44 are strangely attuned to the subsequent atomic era in that they reduce matter to blown vapor. And it is an interesting fact that in 1943 Matta declared his only quarrel with the surrealists was that they disregarded the phenomena of the *physical* sciences. He felt that a new school of painters could evolve from contemporary physics, as an earlier school (surrealism) had evolved from modern psychology.

Surrealism, however, was the main formative influence on Matta's early career, and by 1938 he had so far absorbed its tenets that he had reacted completely away from the concrete, angular order exemplified by Le Corbusier's *machines à habiter*. In that year he published in the surrealist magazine, *Minotaure,* an article, *"Mathématique sensible — Architecture du temps,"* in which the intangible reckonings of psychiatry and time-space replace geometry's solid logic. "Let us," he wrote, "overturn all the historical show-pieces, with their styles and elegant ornamentation, in order that there may escape the rays of dust out of which pyrotechnics can create space . . . We need walls like damp cloths which assume odd shapes and complement our psychological fears." The theory owes much to Dali's previously expressed interest in a malleable architecture, based on Freudian suitability to human needs, but it is nonetheless an interesting forecast of the direction Matta's painting would take.

This direction was soon apparent. By the end of 1938 Matta had painted a number of canvases in which space is created out of gauzes of color and molten forms, like the filmy images cast on a screen by Thomas Wilfred's Clavilux, a light-machine which Matta saw in operation several years later and admired enormously. Matta was not alone, however, in his predilection for a soft, flowing and ambiguous space, since Wolfgang Paalen was then working in a roughly comparable direction, while Yves Tanguy had long since proved himself the ultimate master of what is referred to in film production as the "lap dissolve" — the fading of one image into another, as when Tanguy's earth melts with the sky, leaving no line of demarcation and creating a double infinity of distance. From the rigid squares and cones of cubism, abstract form had moved toward the biomorphism of Arp, Miro and the former cubists themselves. Now, seemingly, it was to abandon living contour for an amorphous projection of inner states of mind and spirit, substituting for Kandinsky's musical analogy a reference to psychotic disturbance and release.

Matta was already, in 1938, an independent and original colorist, and thenceforth he developed rapidly. His first one-man exhibition was held in New York in 1940, and in a foreword to the exhibition catalog Nicolas Calas included an extremely apt quotation from Shelley's *Prometheus Unbound:*

> *Ten thousand involving and involved*
> *Purple and azure, white, green and golden*
> *Sphere within sphere; and every shape between*
> *Peopled with unimaginable shapes.*

The color in Matta's oils of 1938–40 was extremely bright, washed thinly over the canvas, but sometimes congealing into quick jewels of gaudy and variable hue. His forms

MATTA: The Earth Is a Man, 1942. *Oil. 71⅝ x 95⅝". Collection Mr. and Mrs. Henry Clifford, Radnor, Pa.*

were frequently erotic in connotation, though they were never specific or precise. His bold, Latin-American reds, blues, greens and yellows floated with subconscious freedom; they swirled around dead pockets; piled up in hard clusters, like dies spilled on a stream; moved on again in paling color, not only across but into the picture space. Matta was at this time the absolute opposite of those later surrealist artists who painted as realistically as possible in order to give public credence to the unbelievable. His technique was spontaneous to the point of being careless. In some of his paintings of this and a later period, for example, he allowed the pigment to spill and run in certain sections, creating its own accidental patterns.

A certain contempt for medium was a fundamental of Matta's esthetic from the beginning, and was encouraged by his association with the surrealists. Moreover, he has always insisted on a preference for "experienced" as opposed to "theoretical" art, assigning most of cubism and all purely abstract painting to the latter category, his own to the former, and deriving the distinction between the two from a devoted reading of the philosophies of William James and John Dewey. As his own "experience" has become more cohesive and mature, he has worked with new authority. By 1941, the scattered and uneven brilliance of his earlier canvases had gathered into one impressive whole.

Perhaps a trip to Mexico in 1941 hastened his development. Late in 1940 he had begun to vary the candy-stick tonality of his previous paintings by sometimes using a dark, over-all ground, green or blue or red, in which bloomed sudden vivid crocuses of color. He returned from Mexico with renewed interest in the pyrotechnics which his *Minotaure* article had declared could "create space." The heavens in his pictures now exploded in a shower of volcanic sparks and spiraling lava. At the same time, the landscape of Mexico seems to have taught him a more rhythmic relationship between earth and sky, as in the Museum of Modern Art's fine canvas, *Listen to Life*. His burning stones plunged deeper and deeper into an ethereal maze, and he extended space by a labyrinth of diaphanous screens, tissue behind tissue, the light reflecting back and forth, through and between. But he was apparently dissatisfied with this remarkable spatial manipulation, and toward the end of 1941 there occurred a decided break in his style.

He now began to combine his coloristic and amorphous suggestion of space with a use of linear perspective. The experiment was suggested by surrealism's chief, André Breton, and was given form by Giorgio de Chirico's proto-surrealist paintings of 1910– 17, in which strong, architectural lines converge abruptly to suggest a remote distance. In a number of canvases painted in 1941 and 1942, Matta pierced his thin sprays of color with triangular or rectangular corridors, white, solid and heavily lined, leading past walls of flame, or cutting through banked mists of rose, yellow and blue. His dual perspective of color and line was on the whole rather unsuccessful, since the geometric areas broke up his compositions to a degree which no virtuosity of surrounding tonal invention could repair. But 1942 was in any case a year of restless experiment for Matta. He was determined to abandon the beguiling, tropical palette of his vaporish landscapes, and was becoming suspicious of his own moderate popularity. For the most part he now held himself in conscious check, though during the year he completed the large and brilliant *The Earth Is a Man* (page 63), now in the collection of Henry Clifford at Radnor, Pennsylvania. The picture is the climax of his early manner, a summary of everything he intended to leave behind in an eventual search for sterner architectonic order and more specific psychological content.

At this time Matta remarked: "Painting always has one foot in architecture, one foot in the dream." By the fall of 1942 he began temporarily to shift his own weight as a painter toward the dream, though he retained a greater respect for the conventional plastic virtues than he had shown earlier. His rigid Chiricoesque platforms gradually disappeared, and he commenced to cover his smoking colors with a meandering surface calligraphy which had appeared only fitfully in previous works. Two dark pictures painted at the end of the year, a red one entitled *Omega of a Lost Word,* and a blue one

MATTA: A Grave Situation, 1945–46. *Oil, 55 x 77". The Pierre Matisse Gallery, New York.*

called *Acquasapphire,* announced the new direction. Both were inscribed with white lines which floated like threads on the swimming space beneath, sometimes following the movement of the color, but more often running free, like automatic writing. It would be interesting to know whether this new style was partially inspired by the installation designed by Marcel Duchamp for the Surrealist Exhibition which opened at 451 Madison Avenue, New York, on October 14, 1942. Duchamp had strung the huge main gallery of the exhibition with white twine, forming an intricate web around pictures and walls, so that everything was seen through an illusory and changeable third dimension. The installation cannot have failed to impress Matta, who was actively connected with the exhibition. The theory of its effect on his painting is the more plausible in that Duchamp's influence on him has been strong, as we shall see. In any case, Matta's surface calligraphy grew more pervasive in pictures like *Absolute Unity.* Presently he began to vary its loose scribble with precise loop-like forms, and black lines often replaced white.

The lines themselves, whether "free" or planned, were of marked distinction, and perhaps this is the place to speak of Matta's drawing as an independent medium. Long before he attained maturity as a painter, he was producing an astonishing series of drawings in which he evoked from the crayons of children a brilliance of tone usually reserved for pastel. In general spirit, these drawings belonged to the violently sadistic vein of surrealism already explored by André Masson, and through them Matta developed a number of the iconographical motifs which were to appear in his paintings in more generalized or amorphous form. Gradually, however, his drawings became virtually paintings, so rich was their use of color; and their subject matter often followed a more or less separate track toward the creation of a fantastic bestiary. In 1942 he began to use occasionally the comic-strip technique of presenting images in succession on a single sheet. Picasso, once described by Gertrude Stein as in youth a great admirer of American comics, had previously used the technique in his magnificent drawings for *The Dream and Lie of Franco*. There can be no doubt that Matta followed his example, particularly since his own drawings were often of a comparable scatologic intensity. Yet Matta's comic-strips and his other drawings are extremely original in style, and have already exerted a considerable influence of their own on American artists of his and an older generation.

In 1943 Matta completed the second of his large-scale canvases, *The Convict of Light*. The picture reflects the special alarm of that year of war; it portrays a chaotic firmament, filled with colliding planes, fire rising and falling, drifting fogs and zodiacal signs. Late in the same year, he attempted another solution of the perspective problem, turning away from de Chirico's linear system toward the mechano-morphology of Marcel Duchamp's huge glass, *The Bride Stripped Bare by Her Bachelors* (1915–23). One of Matta's earlier canvases, *Fire* (1941), had included a structure of crossbars reminiscent of the watermill section in the lower half of Duchamp's glass; his *Years of Fear* (1942) had utilized a weathervane form which recalls the upper panel of Duchamp's composition. Now, in the late fall of 1943, he painted *The Bachelors Twenty Years Later* in open tribute to Duchamp.

Thenceforth Matta was to draw at intervals on both the morphological and the mechanical spatial techniques of Duchamp. *The Bride Stripped Bare by Her Bachelors* has remained a central force in the formation of his recent esthetic, and may have inspired the interest in multiple-panel compositions which led him at this period to create a number of triptychs in varying sizes. Duchamp and Matta have been close and devoted friends. The older painter has several times remarked that for him Matta is the only very young painter of great talent visible anywhere. And Matta's reverence for Duchamp is understandable: what other twentieth-century work of art combines "architecture and the dream" more distinctly than the latter's *The Bride?*

At this point in his career, Matta appears to have felt the need for re-exploring the great trends of the late nineteenth and early twentieth centuries, and one of his 1944 paintings was entitled *Cézanne's Apples,* while another unexpectedly resumed the problems of cubism's structure. But then, through one of those revulsions of spirit which are

66

inevitable in a man of Matta's restless and energetic temperament, he came abruptly to an end of disciplinary retrospection. During the early spring of 1944 he painted one of the outstanding and most personal works of his career to date — the large *Vertige d'Eros,* in the Museum of Modern Art collection.* The picture is extraordinary in its evocation of an inexplicable mythology of forms, emerging and receding in deepest space. The canvas engulfs the spectator to a curious degree, arousing a sensation of dream projection quite unlike the usual esthetic response. Within the composition, illusion leads to illusion, as in a superb water carnival where the darkness flares with mysterious activity, far off or near, veiled in haunting ambiguity. What are the objects shown? Matta himself has prepared iconographical charts of several of his large-scale works, but these, though they elucidate his philosophical sources, contribute little to tangible recognition beyond what we ourselves can supply — floating stones, a fire of twigs, a phallus, a bomb burst, an equivocal over-all sky writing. Until clinical evidence in such matters is far more detailed than at present, perhaps we can do no more than describe Matta as an impressionist of the subconscious mind's eerie light and shadows and forms.

During this same spring of 1944 Matta completed a folio of eleven etchings which announced a further departure in his art. He had previously spoken of his interest in exploring climactic stages of emotion, and had conceived the unlikely project of persuading the military authorities to fly him over battle areas so that he might record his paroxysms of fear. He turned in his etchings to orgiastic scenes, portraying figures which were of a frightening obscenity, but powerful, obsessive and convinced. He often mentioned at this time his admiration for Grünewald's "turning forms," and from the intertwined fingers of the Virgin and saints in the German master's Isenheim altarpiece, he probably drew a good part of his inspiration for the laced figures in his etchings. The influence applies not only to his prints, but to the paintings in related vein which he produced late in 1944 and early in 1945; it may be traced at its most specific in the *Man Trembling.*

The paintings in the 1944–45 series abandon the romantic auras of his early canvases for a vigorous, primarily linear depiction of psychological states and monstrous action. The theme of many is erotic, though less so than in the etchings. But unlike Miro's sexual preoccupation, which Matta once described as "popular eroticism," Matta's imagery is presented in terms of a psychotic symbology, unrelenting in its ferocity and complication. It is worth noting, however, that Matta himself has occasionally made use of "popular" sources. The prickled, hairy arms of certain recent figures are akin to those of

* Matta has inherited the extreme interest in titles of pictures which Duchamp, Max Ernst and de Chirico revived for our century. A note on the title of this picture may therefore be of interest. It was inspired by Freud's statement that all realization falls between Eros and the instant of death. Matta called his picture *Le Vertige d'Eros* ("The Vertigo of Eros"). But when he mentioned the title to a friend, the friend repeated it to him as *La Verte Tige des Roses* ("The Green Stem of the Roses"). The pun had not been intended by Matta, but he was delighted with it, and described it as a "realized" rather than an "invented" pun, that is, one brought about by accidental usage rather than made up.

Pop-Eye the Sailor Man, while Matta's suggestion of motion by the use of vibrating, hatched lines is perhaps directly evolved from a familiar comic-strip technique.

During the spring of 1946 Matta exhibited in New York the paintings he had completed early that year and late in 1945. In them the erotic tumult of the previous year has relaxed somewhat, and at the same time they show greater technical assurance and care. Two of these works, *Anxiety in Trompe l'Oeil* and *Being With,* reveal in relatively pure and abstract form the continuing influence of Duchamp's big glass, an influence which extends to other pictures of the series. Yet Matta has created a new *ambiance* for Duchamp's crystalline handling of mechanical perspective. He has evolved a sultry, mustard-colored nether world, furnished with a sort of imaginary modern office equipment, as though his memories of Le Corbusier's office had returned to him in nightmare guise. And in the most impressive paintings of the new series, he retains the large-scale demonic image in quasi-human form to which he had first turned in a painting of 1944–45, entitled *A Poet.* In *A Grave Situation* (page 65), *The Argumouth, Chambole-les-amoureuses* and the huge panel, *The Splitting of the Ergo,* Matta peoples his world of glass tables and labyrinthine gadgets with monstrous figures, screaming, hurtling through space, their hands convulsed and knotted, exhibiting a crisis of nerves in a surrounding of fantastic antisepsis. These are figures of almost Germanic violence, not unrelated to Max Ernst's chimerical beings; their torment is inexplicable but agonizingly real. They have emerged from the bedroom which was their milieu in 1944–45 to face grave upheavals in the outer world. They argue, they are attacked, they implore, they torture. One of them, in *Jittering the Feelings,* defines their emotional state by clutching his exposed nerves in a gesture of despair and foreboding.

What direction will Matta's art take now? Nothing can be predicted, for it has been his courageous habit to abandon ruthlessly styles which he feels he has exhausted. His energy and pictorial imagination seem boundless, and for so young a man he has already produced a remarkable body of work. From the tinted quicksilver of his early landscapes to the horrendous demonology of his recent paintings, is a long and drastic journey of the imagination. We may well ask what other artist of his generation has come so far and so boldly on the road which the surrealists rediscovered twenty-odd years ago.

SOME YOUNGER AMERICAN PAINTERS

What new American painters have emerged during the past few years, what is their quality and importance? In attempting to answer such questions, one sins openly with conjecture. The period is too recent for anything like careful evaluation; it is ripe only for tentative, personal opinion, for a journalistic account of the younger Americans whose work has appeared conspicuously in New York during the time, not yet ended, when that city has been the most active art center in the world.

It must be said, to begin with, that the three great movements of our century — expressionism, abstraction and surrealism — have pointed the way, separately or in combination, for many of the newer American painters. Expressionism has been an especially powerful force, though we still have no better definition of its premise than was provided by Rouault's master, Gustave Moreau, before the movement was formally launched. "Art," said Moreau, "is a furious tracking down of the inner feelings solely by means of plastic expression." The progenitors of expressionism, of course, were the early Cézanne, van Gogh, Gauguin, Ferdinand Hodler and Edvard Munch, followed by the German artists of The Bridge and The Blue Rider and by the French *fauves,* followed still later by the melancholy and fevered Lithuanian, Chaim Soutine. For certain young Americans the example of Rouault and Soutine has been particularly important, and in Boston about ten years ago there appeared two very young painters, Jack Levine and Hyman Bloom, who found in these masters a point of departure toward bravura styles which were notable for sincerity of emotion as well as exceptional fluency.

The appearance of Levine and Bloom in Boston was a heartening phenomenon, an indication that the thinning forces of Anglo-Saxon gentility were being replenished by Baltic emigration, in art at least. Both painters studied at the Boston Museum's art school, where both were inspired by the theories and personality of Dr. Denman Ross. But there were important differences between the two young men, both personal and professional. Levine was born in this country in 1915, and his earliest years were spent in the slums of Boston's South End. When he was eight, his family moved to a residential suburb and, characteristically, Levine later described himself as "horrified by [its] trees and piazzas." Thus he is by instinct and formative childhood memory a painter of the American city's oppressive squalor, of its vigor, color and terrifying inequalities. And though his small pictures of Old Testament figures, executed around 1940, are among the most distinguished works produced by his generation, his true field is satire, opulently handled, with broad, flashing brushstrokes and sumptuous color (page 70). His *Feast of Pure Reason,* painted when he was only twenty-two, is already, I think, something of a landmark in modern American painting. It has helped bury the exhausted theory that American artists misunderstand or fear the sensual qualities of pigment, and

Jack LEVINE: Welcome Home, 1946. *Oil, 40 x 60″. The Brooklyn Museum, New York.*

proved that Rembrandt is now as available a part of our artists' heritage as Claude Lorrain or the taut perfectionists of nineteenth-century realism. Since that brilliant beginning, Levine has completed a series of satirical pictures in which his technique has become steadily more deft, even dazzling, so that his struggle now is against virtuosity itself rather than against Puritan leanness of means. But he knows the dangers of richness-for-its-own-sake, and his paintings retain a bitter rind of conviction. Moreover, Soutine's starfish hands and bat-eared heads no longer appear in his works, and he is more than ever his own master.

Bloom is a different matter. Born in Latvia in 1913 and brought to Boston as a child, he has disregarded the passing scene, and has returned to those ancient cloisters of the mind where men are concerned with religious symbolism, with death, putrefaction and the vicissitudes of the spirit. During the late 1930's, when his career began, he painted an astonishing series of synagogue interiors, filling every inch of them with the solemn, luxurious clutter of ritual — wry-necked cantors, choirboys, bearded rabbis, torahs and swaying chandeliers. His gods then were the mosaicists of Ravenna, Caravaggio, Rem-

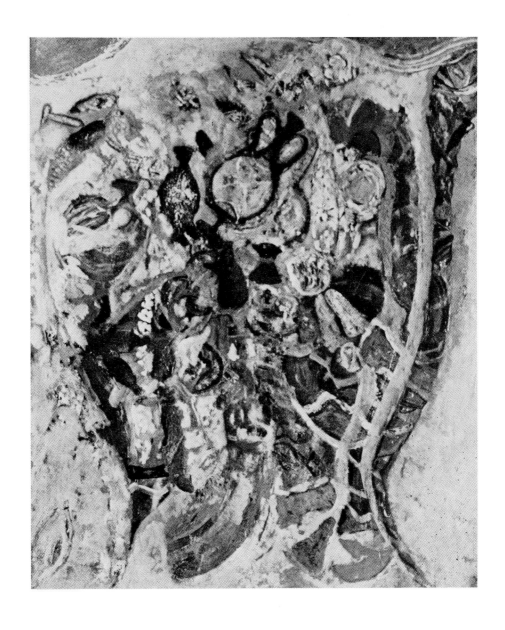

Hyman BLOOM: Archeological Treasure, 1945. *Oil, 43 x 36″. Collection Edgar Kauf-mann, Jr., New York.*

Robert MOTHERWELL: Construction, 1946–47. *Oil, 72 x 54". The Samuel Kootz Gallery, New York.*

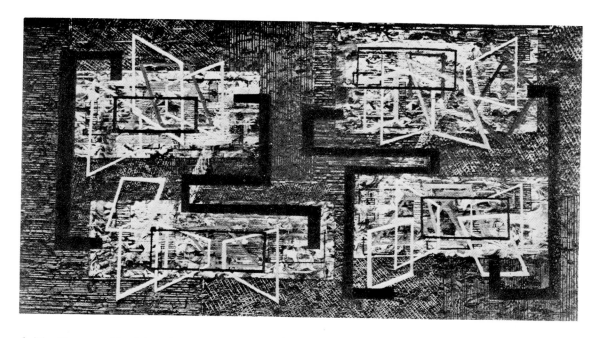

I. Rice Pereira: Quadrigraph, 1945. *Oil, 16 x 30". Collection Mr. and Mrs. Holger Cahill, New York.*

brandt, Blake, Rouault, Chagall, Soutine and Paul Klee. Gradually his vision burned to a narrower flame, and he painted single figures with torahs or huge canvases of a chandelier whose burnished surfaces reflected in evasive concentrate the pageantry below. Then, a year or so ago, Bloom began to paint near-abstractions, visceral in derivation, but lyric and tender (page 71). Accompanying these pictures were several images of bloated corpses and severed limbs, recalling the superb studies that Théodore Géricault made in the early nineteenth century for his masterwork, *The Raft of the Medusa.* These are frightening pictures admittedly, but they are dignified by their passion, and we must not forget that such subjects appealed to many great artists of the past until, in turn, Rococo gaiety and Victorian prudery ruled them aside. In any case, Bloom remains one of the most inspired artists of the new generation, and whatever he does is worth our respectful attention.

Levine and Bloom have been followed lately by a third Boston expressionist, David Aronson. Born in Latvia in 1923, Aronson, like Bloom, paints religious-symbolic subjects (he studied formal religion for eight years), and I do not know why it is that he tends to slickness even when his intention is reverent or fierce. But he has painted one or two distinguished works; he is still very young, and he shares with Levine and Bloom a precociousness which has not harmed them and may not harm him.

The two strong currents of expressionism and abstraction have often merged during the past thirty years, producing in combination some of the most interesting younger artists in this country. In the autumn of 1943, for example, Jackson Pollock was given

73

Jackson POLLOCK: The She-Wolf, 1943. *Oil, 41⅞ x 67". The Museum of Modern Art, New York.*

his first one-man exhibition at the Art of This Century in New York, and it was immediately apparent that here was a painter of very considerable expressive power, daring, undisciplined and strong. Born in Wyoming in 1912, Pollock studied for a time under Thomas Benton, but gravitated finally to the New York studio of Hans Hofmann, German born, who had long since brought to a predominantly non-representational art the slashing brushwork and heavy impasto of Central European expressionism. Pollock progressed rapidly under Hofmann's tutelage; his first exhibition revealed him, not as an artist of promise, but as one of mature accomplishment, and to date I have not seen a finer picture by him than the *She-Wolf* of 1943 (above). Most conspicuous of his virtues was his headlong Baroque exuberance, his willingness to forego calculation and the niceties of balance in favor of primary emotional impact. His intimacy with the oil medium was rapt and without caution; he worked fluently and quickly in large scale; his line had something of Picasso's audacious certainty; his spattered color was luminous, variable and deep. Then, for a time, his remarkable energy seemed to become too dispersed and loose, and the limitations of his organizational sense grew disturbingly ob-

74

Adolph GOTTLIEB: Voyager's Return, 1946. *Oil, $37\frac{7}{8}$ x $29\frac{7}{8}$". The Museum of Modern Art, New York. Gift of Mr. and Mrs. Roy R. Neuberger.*

vious. Lately, however, he has gained new momentum, and perhaps he will yet wring out of restraint the conviction he once enjoyed because he was both reckless and swift.

Cubism and its later, abstract developments continue to exert a tremendous influence among younger American painters. Indeed we may one day discover abstraction's reign to have been longest in America, for in France the neo-cubists must combat a revived interest in the more decorative problems posed years ago by Bonnard and Matisse, while in England the younger painters are turning back to native romantic traditions. In Italy many of the new men are engrossed in social realism — a theme whose relevance to art had previously been denied there more persistently than elsewhere. But in America ab-

Theodore STAMOS: Sounds in the Rock, 1947. *Oil, 48⅛ x 28⅜″.* **The Museum** *of Modern Art, New York. Gift of Edward W. Root.*

William BAZIOTES: Dwarf, 1947. *Oil, 42 x 36⅛". The Museum of Modern Art, New York.*

straction goes on, most brilliantly, perhaps, at the hands of I. Rice Pereira (page 73). It has lately attracted the two young painters, Robert Motherwell (b. 1915) and William Baziotes (b. 1911), who have paid particular heed to the *collage* and to those aspects of abstract art which touch on the enigmatic and in which there lingers some hint of humanist reference (page 72 and above). Both men work with startling assurance and, seeing their work, the French painter Fernand Léger is said to have remarked that it had taken him many, many years to learn as much as they already knew. Motherwell in fact works with such professional flair that we instinctively ask: is he as good as he seems? Personally I find that many of his pictures create an excitement which does not always hold on second look. But he is spontaneous, able and courageous, not at all stylish, and the next few years should decide whether he is a first-rate artist or an extremely skillful commentator on earlier twentieth-century abstract trends. Baziotes, I think, is progressing more surely. He is not as witty as Motherwell nor as beguiling, but richness and cohesion begin to ap-

Mark ROTHKO: Archaic Idol, 1945. *Watercolor, 19½ x 26¼". Collection Kenneth MacPherson, New York.*

pear simultaneously in his works. What promises most in his art is its direct relation to experience, for at this late date in abstraction's course, the disembodied exercise is more common than the expression of inner need. Perhaps every good picture, whether abstract or not, must have an element of confession, and Baziotes' paintings, being hard-fought and real, escape the limitations of improvisation on an assumed theme. The painter himself has said: "There is always a subject in my mind that is more important than anything else. Sometimes I am aware of it, sometimes not."

Three painters of very roughly related tendency are Adolph Gottlieb (b. 1903), Mark Rothko (b. Russia, 1903) and Theodore Stamos (b. 1922). For some years Gottlieb has devoted himself to the pictograph — the segmental presentation of symbolic forms, as in ancient and primitive art and in the contemporary paintings of the Uruguayan, Torres García. I used to feel that Gottlieb's symbols were too archaistic and lacking in meaningful continuity, but in such a work as the recent *Voyager's Return* (page 75) he has attained new unity and finer color, a skillful placing of his component forms.

Mark Rothko's is a different temperament. However non-representational he may be, he belongs fundamentally, I think, to the "sensibility" tradition which has flourished at various times in various countries. His painting is gracious, sensitive and lyric (opposite), so that he has affinities of spirit, if not of subject, with modern Venetian painters like De Pisis, whose work he may not know at all.

Of the painters thus far mentioned in this chapter the youngest is Theodore Stamos. His painting belongs to the vein of organic abstraction of which the late Arthur Dove was perhaps the most consistent American exponent, and is akin to the art of William Baziotes, who is also of Greek ancestry. Stamos is already quite clearly a painter of exceptional talent and depth, and one feels in his work the same ardent communion with nature that characterizes the art of the Englishman, Graham Sutherland. His broad, warm forms, mysterious and hardy, express in contemporary terms the romantic naturalism which has been a persistent element in American art, and it is perhaps no accident that his most enthusiastic patron is Mr. Edward W. Root, who long ago discovered the early watercolors of Charles Burchfield. Stamos' *Sounds in the Rock* (page 76) seems to me a distinguished picture for so young an artist.

Surrealism appears to be dying out as a formal movement in this country, though its rejuvenation of art's imaginative faculties remains a major and pervasive contribution, and has affected many younger American artists, most directly Jimmy Ernst, Clyfford Still and Charles Seliger. But realism — the oldest and most continuous of American pictorial traditions — is today perhaps more varied in application than ever before in this country. There is, for instance, the still-life painter, Walter Tandy Murch (b. 1907), who portrays strange broken instruments of time and weather, and has developed an unusually luminous technique (page 80). No one can predict what fame Murch will enjoy in his lifetime, his art being quiet in an era of blare, but I can imagine later generations coming on his pictures excitedly, as we now come on those of the nineteenth-century realist, William Harnett. And with Alton Pickens (b. 1917), realism flares off toward the heady, tormented mysticism of early sixteenth-century German painting — an uncommon source of inspiration for American artists. Many people are repelled by Pickens' images of violent, tragic, deformed children; I find them brave, genuine and compelling. Moreover, there are few young painters anywhere — Balthus in France and Francis Bacon in England are among them — with so powerful a gift for intensifying reality in the direction of the macabre (page 81). In the Pickens *Blue Doll*, for example, children on a New York street are burning their dolls — a scene which Pickens actually witnessed. But these aged waifs appear as agents of a horrendous witchcraft, sinister, disturbing, violent in gesture and grimace, yet exhibiting that compulsive force which separates terror from mere emotional titillation.

Honoré Sharrer's realism focuses on contemporary American life, but she stares so intently at its details that an almost chimerical scene results, half stage and half parlor, pantomime and actuality existing evocatively together. In 1944 Mr. Lincoln Kirstein brought to New York from West Point a little picture, *Workers and Paintings* (page 84)

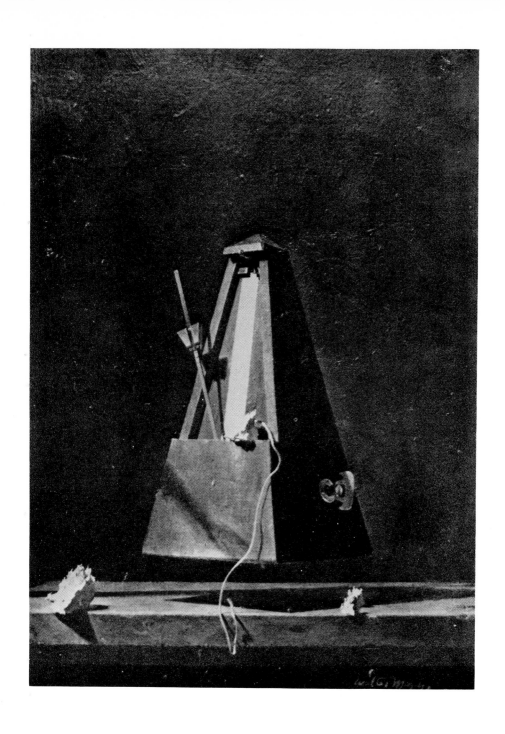

Walter Tandy MURCH: The Metronome, 1946. *Oil, 21¼ x 15¼". Collection James Caffrey, New York.*

Alton PICKENS: The Acrobat, 1947. *Oil, 50 x 34". The Buchholz Gallery, New York.*

Walter STUEMPFIG: The Wall, 1946. *Oil, 31½ x 40½". The Pennsylvania Academy of Fine Arts, Philadelphia.*

which Miss Sharrer had completed as a study for a mural. The painting seems to me one of the most notable images achieved by a younger American artist, its iconographic invention and technical skill so marked, its humanism so sympathetic and acute, that it sticks in memory in full detail. The picture celebrates Miss Sharrer's two principal preoccupations — art and American workers; it does so with inventive variety of observation and statement. Born in 1920 and now living in New York, Miss Sharrer has since worked mainly on panels for triptychs on the theme of working-class American life. The best of these are comparable in quality to *Workers and Paintings,* but occasionally there now appears in her art a note of rather perversely elegant fantasy.

Allied to Miss Sharrer in the attempt to intensify the American scene through imaginative interpretation is Walter Stuempfig (b. 1914), though he crosses over into romantic territory, as did so many of our earlier realists on occasion. Stuempfig belongs by heritage and training to the Philadelphia tradition in art to which I have already referred in the chapter on Charles Demuth. His art is notable for an instinctive elegance and a flair for pictorial order, so that without apparent effort he endows an American

Stephen GREENE: The Deposition, 1947. *Oil, 59 x 34". Collection Joseph Pulitzer, Jr., St. Louis.*

Honoré SHARRER: Workers and Paintings, 1943. *Oil, 11⅝ x 37". The Museum of Modern Art, New York. Gi̟*
Lincoln Kirstein.

summer resort such as Cape May, New Jersey, with the nostalgic charm and dignity of
the old European spas. His painterly gifts are so decided, indeed, that he has had to
fight down a weakness for Grand Style flourish. An extremely conscientious artist, he
had lately given his pictures a more vital substance, perhaps looking away from Poussin
toward our modern Edward Hopper, not in confusion, but out of the sound belief that
he needs the present's sharp profile as much as the past's atmospheric veil (page 82).

One of the most promising developments in recent American art is the use of extreme
realism in conjunction with broad, abstract tensions of design, derived as often from the
mid-fifteenth-century masters of static balance — especially Piero della Francesca and
Uccello — as from Picasso, Klee and other artists of our own period. The tendency
sounds eclectic, as does nearly every new approach to art until someone makes it work.
Ben Shahn has done precisely this for more than fifteen years, and now has attracted an
impressive young recruit in Stephen Greene (b. 1918). Of course there is danger as
well as promise in this direction, for the Renaissance can smother its modern disciples
with quotations, and it is no easy task to inject realism into the very arteries of twentieth-
century abstraction. But Shahn has long since succeeded superbly, and there is every
indication that Greene, like Shahn, will acquire a protective toughness of mind. He
begins to do so in *The Deposition* (page 83).

These, then, are *some* of the newer American artists. I wonder what would have been
said of them by that mid-nineteenth-century European landscapist who strode off the
boat at New York and briskly inquired: "And now where is the sketching ground?"
The American sketching ground is three thousand miles from sea to sea. Once, this was
a disadvantage for our artists, struggling with the wilderness and isolation. In this
century, I think, it begins to account for the energy, variety and promise of our younger
painters.

84

MAX BECKMANN

Of the German expressionists whose careers began in the opening years of this century, only Max Beckmann of those who have survived paints today with undiminished vigor. Indeed, in the 1939 triptych here reproduced (page 87), and in a number of paintings executed during and since the recent war, he has achieved some of his finest works. His late pictures are remarkable for a continuing liveliness of pictorial invention, for technical mastery, and especially for a depth of conviction which only a few artists of our century have been able to maintain over so long a period.

Beckmann was born in Leipzig in 1884, and was trained at the Weimar Academy. In 1906 he joined the famous Berlin Secession, then dominated by Max Liebermann and by the agitated variant of French impressionism that Liebermann, Lovis Corinth and Max Slevogt had developed in Germany. Beckmann's choice of allegiance was conservative, for a more advanced trend in painting was already being explored by the artists of *Die Brücke*, whose three founders were strict contemporaries of Beckmann (Schmidt-Rottluff was exactly his age, Heckel a year and Kirchner three years older). By 1904 the painters of *Die Brücke* had discovered African and Oceanic sculpture, and were seeking to overthrow the ideals of impressionism by following the precepts of Gauguin and van Gogh. Beckmann, on the other hand, painted a recognizably impressionist work as late as 1911, while during part of his early career he alternated between stormy landscapes in the Liebermann-Corinth vernacular and portraits stemming from later nineteenth-century German realism.

From the evidence of other paintings executed by Beckmann between 1905 and 1911, however, it is clear that wilder ambitions were smoldering within him, ignited perhaps by the frenzied art of Lovis Corinth, whose brutal strength often turned impressionism convulsive. Indeed, Corinth is sometimes described as Beckmann's master at the Weimar Academy, but this is not true; in reply to a recent inquiry on this point, Beckmann replied that he had never studied under Corinth but that he and his companions had all worked separately and independently (*"sonst alles allein"*). In any case, Beckmann's own dynamism showed first in his love of complicated iconography — a significant fact, since Beckmann is one of the few contemporary painters whose subject matter must be a major factor in our estimate of his powers. Whereas his greatly gifted countryman, Franz Marc, was content to be an *animalier,* though of an intensely subjective kind, Beckmann has brought even to still-life painting a textual excitement fairly uncommon in modern art as a whole. Throughout his career he has stressed the importance of allegory, emblems and parables, so that he may one day seem to iconographers a particularly rewarding subject for research.

During his formative years Beckman is said to have worshipped Tintoretto, and among his early works are several large figure compositions which reflect the tensions of the Venetian's style. He is also said to have admired Delacroix, and a few of his paintings of 1905–12 share the great romantic's interest in a grandiose dramaturgy which the evolution of European art since the seventeenth century had tended, with exceptions, to leave behind. Indeed there are Beckmanns of the early period in which Delacroix's romantic defiance is resumed in more riotous and savage form, and one feels from the evidence of Hans Kaiser's astonishingly early monograph (1913), that the young German painter instinctively resisted the modern preference for the sharp fragment over the convoluted whole.

Even in youth Beckmann was often concerned with symbolism and metaphysical content — those constants of his mature vision — and we find in one or two of his pictures of 1906–08 a cabalistic fantasy which foretells what was to come. He was then already fond of contrasts between realistic and metaphorical motifs; his *Auferstehung* of 1908–09, with its vertical compression and interplay of allegorical and contemporary figures, prophecies the merger of fact with fable which takes place frequently in his later works. Even those early paintings which are more plainly lyric in conception, lead directly to recent pictures in the same relaxed vein. As an extreme example, a figure in his *Young Men by the Sea* of 1905 reappears, almost intact, in one of the most gracious of his late paintings, the *Young Men at the Coast* of 1943.

If the young Beckmann for a time combined Grand Style ideology with late nineteenth-century technical formulas, he moved forward around 1912 into the main stream of advanced Central European art. There then began to appear in his painting signs of expressionism's wracking malaise, probably through the influence of the Norwegian, Edvard Munch, rather than of Beckmann's countrymen, though in 1911 Kandinsky and Marc had launched *Der Blaue Reiter* which, far more persuasively than *Die Brücke*, focused attention on subjective ways of seeing and sealed the doom of impressionism as a living force for younger German artists.

Inspired by whatever source, Beckmann began to simplify his figure compositions and to replace their Mannerist-Baroque congestion of forms with a few bold motifs, defined by harsh contours and strong color. The change in his style is startlingly revealed by a comparison between his *Adam and Eve* of 1907 and the version of the same subject which he both etched and painted ten years later. The former picture shows two academic figures in an interior hung with garlands of flowers; its spirit is decidedly nineteenth century, and its heavy idealism might have been conceived by several painters of an earlier generation. The 1917 etching and painting, on the other hand, are violently stark images, as forceful in condensation as fifteenth-century German woodcuts; the gestures of the figures are savagely expressive; the decorative flowers of the 1907 version have been abandoned, and in their place appears a serpent with the mask of a wolf — a characteristic Beckmann monster. Beckmann was now fully abreast of the expressionist tendency, both as to economy of means and as to emphasis on a barbaric emotionalism.

Self portraits of artists are often important documents of their psychological develop-

Max BECKMANN: Acrobats (triptych), 1939. *Oil, 78½″ high, wings 35⅝″ wide, central panel 67″ wide. Collection Wright Ludington, Santa Barbara.*

ment. This seems especially true of Beckmann, who has reported his own appearance at frequent intervals, with utter frankness, in many media. Thus in 1909 he had executed a double portrait of himself and wife, and therein appears as a sensitive, professorial young man of marked assurance and respectability. In 1917, however, he painted himself as a tormented, solitary artist, animal-like in the ferocity of his reaction to the wartime chaos, a snarling figure fighting for his existence as a creative painter. He had served in the German army, and the horrors of his experience had acted as a tremendous catalytic, as in the case of his contemporary and countryman, George Grosz. Released from military service in 1917, Beckmann went to live in Frankfort and to teach in the Academy there. Over the next two years, he produced a number of paintings in which his anguish is conveyed with mounting power. His *Descent from the Cross* of 1917 is one of the memorable religious pictures of our time, its impact so fierce that we are reminded of the early sixteenth-century Germanic tradition which included Grünewald, Altdorfer and Ratgeb. Yet the angularity of Beckmann's painting is perhaps more closely related to the earlier, Gothic style in the North, and it seems probable that at this time he drew inspiration from the sculpture and graphic art of the Middle Ages in Germany, as well as from fifteenth-century native painters, notably those who had centered in the Rhenish district of Franconia and there had evolved a tremendously tough and realistic style. In 1917 Beckmann also completed a *Christ and the Adulteress* in which is evinced, possibly for the first time, his abiding concern with mockery as a basic psychological theme. The clownish figure deriding Christ in this picture is the prototype of numerous jesters whose screeching inanity echoes through many of Beckmann's later compositions. The torment of the war years, as suffered by the artist, reached its climax in an almost pathologically bitter and gruesome work, *The Night,* painted in 1918–19.

During the early 1920's, Beckmann's color, which had previously held to a restrained and brownish tonality, became rich and varied. He then painted several fantasies in an exaggeratedly vertical format (he has frequently chosen canvases whose odd dimensions add to the shock of the images, and are a calculated part of his plastic intention). These pictures were widely reproduced, particularly *Circus* and *Crazy House,* and greatly extended his fame. The two paintings mentioned are related in spirit, if obliquely, to the cynicism of the Dada movement, which found man's ambitions ludicrous, his dignity pompous and deceptive, but which revived hope, nonetheless, through the very vigor of its scorn. Beckmann's *Circus* and *Crazy House* are not viciously distraught, as was *The Night;* they do not accuse, as did the *Descent from the Cross.* Their chimerical action takes place within the realm of professionally contrived fantasy — in a circus dressing room and in a sideshow, as their titles imply. But the clowns are uncontrollably clownish, the inhabitants of the "mad house" seem truly mad. Indeed, the figures in both pictures behave with fantastic abandon, blowing horns, wearing masks, holding puppets, surrounded by noise-making apparatus and enigmatic objects, related to each other by their absorption in an over-all lunacy, but each intent on his own meaningless activity. The grief of the war was over; its aftermath was hysteria, exhibitionism and a pervading sense of futility.

In an etching of c. 1920 the artist depicted himself as a bewildered man in a derby hat, staring straight ahead, as if hypnotized by the antics of the postwar world. At this time he developed the figure style by which we know him most clearly. He adopted, for example, what was to become a recurrent compositional device: the use of sprawled, seated or up-ended foreground figures as the base for a steeply vertical pyramid of bodies. And whereas the metaphysical preoccupations of his Italian contemporary, Giorgio de Chirico, led that artist to stress the relationship between near objects and a vast receding space, Beckmann deliberately flattened his perspective, so that his figures are squeezed upwards and against each other, like climbers on the side of a cliff. The figures themselves, however, are sculptural in handling, and are given unity by a skillful cross-stitching of their contours. Throughout his career Beckmann has returned to the problem of extreme plasticity within a relief formula, and on this subject his own words are decidedly relevant: "Height, width and depth are the three phenomena which I must transfer into one plane to form the abstract surface of the picture, and thus to protect myself from the infinity of space." And again: "To transform three into two dimensions is for me an experience full of magic in which I glimpse for a moment that fourth dimension which my whole being is seeking." The heir to Northern Gothic, he has usually placed his figures on the shallow stage that vaudeville performers use while the

88

Max BECKMANN: Four Men around the Table, 1943. *Oil, 58⅜ x 45¼". Washington University, St. Louis.*

full set of a production is being made ready. Against this near curtain, his actors achieve an illogical but haunting tableau, an acrobatic structure of living forms.

At this same period Beckmann evolved a dramatic art of still-life painting to which a certain mystery of assortment and a cacophonous orchestration of color supply an extremely idiosyncratic character. He began, too, to paint city landscapes, using a zig-zag treatment of space in which harsh planes pull against each other with explosive force, but are relieved by those rounded elements which assume such varied guise in his art — appearing as mosques, balls, pottery, street lamps, above all as musical horns and candlesticks. He is certainly more interesting as a figure and still-life painter than as a landscapist. Even so, it must be admitted that his landscapes are exceptionally well integrated within his fundamental identity of style, and are not undertaken merely as a relief from more absorbing problems.

By the mid-1920's, the public reaction to the disasters of war had found an outlet in giddy pleasures and extravagance, and for a time Beckmann recorded in his own way the epoch's hedonistic excitement. Here, once more, we must remark the painter's sensitivity to the changing temper of his times: there is a decided shift in spirit between his pictures of c. 1920 and those executed later in the decade. His color became more and more luxurious, sometimes exotic. He now painted people gathered in bars or in ballrooms or at fashionable beaches, and in 1927 he finished one of the most memorable of his self portraits in which he appears as a figure in evening clothes, hand on hip, a suave witness to the sophistication of a reckless society. If some of his paintings of this period are devastatingly satirical, they are not vindicative or ferocious, as were the images of George Grosz. It is as though Beckmann found his subjects amusingly idiotic. The men and women in *The Boat* (1926) and *The Beach* (1927) gesticulate inanely, vacuous but harmless. They do no good nor evil; they merely exhibit themselves.

As an accompaniment to Beckmann's new mood of tolerance, the tensions of his earlier style tended to lose themselves in arabesques of form beneath luminous surfaces, and the psychological content of his figure painting became less insistent. Yet during the 1920's Beckmann completed some of his most piercing portraits, feeling perhaps that if it was useless to lecture an irresponsible society, it was still important to tell the truth about individuals. Toward the end of the decade he lived in Paris for several years. There his painting grew more and more assured and gracious, and for a time seemed in danger of falling into a rather repetitious lyricism, handsome, gifted and strong, but inclined toward mere signature. The 1930's lay ahead.

In 1937 Beckmann moved to Holland, where he has lived ever since. His art had irritated the Nazi authorities at an early date, and his pictures had begun to disappear from the many German museums which owned them (who, having seen it, can forget the magnificent group of Beckmanns formerly in the museum at Frankfort). His flight was inevitable. Before he left Germany, however, he completed what seems to me to be one of the major works of art our century has thus far produced — the triptych, *Departure*, in the Museum of Modern Art collection. The triptych was smuggled out of Germany by inscribing on its back the title *Scenes from Shakespeare's "Tempest."* Its wings tell in symbolic language a story of despair, torture and foreboding; the central panel shows figures embarking in a boat for free lands. The iconographic evolution of the wings stems from Beckmann's paintings of the First World War, and we may also discover motifs used or suggested during the 1920's and early 1930's: a trussed figure with severed hands, already used in *Crazy House* of 1920; a bound, crouched, half-naked woman, the subject of a picture executed in Paris toward 1930, and now the victim of a more final sadism; a still life of fruit, large as the human figures and inexplicably part of their ordeal; a masked figure carrying a fish — one of Beckmann's most persistent emblems; a couple bound by ropes, the woman bearing the sagging weight of her inverted companion. The radiant central panel, though allied to previous beach scenes in luminosity and brilliance of tone, is miraculous in its capacity to express through its upright, stalwart protagonists the resurgence of hope and the relief of escape from persecution. The triptych has often hung in the Museum of Modern Art on the same floor with Picasso's *Guernica*. Between them, the two so different works furnish proof that modern art's symbolism can be as forceful, moving and impressive as anything produced in earlier centuries.

Throughout the war Beckmann hid from the Nazi authorities in Amsterdam. In 1945 word arrived that he was safe, and in the spring of 1946 his paintings of the war years were exhibited in New York. They caused a considerable and deserved excitement, not because they were conspicuously new in style or content but because they were clearly the work of an important painter who had maintained his powers by a superhuman effort of concentration, under appallingly difficult circumstances.

Perhaps the most brilliant work in the exhibition, though others rivaled it closely, was the triptych, *Acrobats,* here reproduced (page 87). The left panel of this triptych is among the most inventive of Beckmann's paintings, and the right and central panels are exceptionally rich both technically and in iconography. The left panel exemplifies with special clarity the artist's lifelong preoccupation with a two-dimensional manipulation of space. At no point in the picture is our eye carried far back by conventional linear perspective. Instead we climb space vertically, as one climbs a ladder, looking straight ahead at the love-making acrobats, downwards at the woman with the parrot, and upwards at the figure on a trapeze. Yet the spatial tension between the figures is so strong that we envision them all at once, effortlessly. In the other two panels the figures are presented frontally, but in them, too, occur arbitrary dislocations of scale — the clown in the right panel clutching a champagne bottle larger than himself, the diminutive boy with drum at the feet of the towering woman in Indian boots. The color is everywhere fresh and rich.

No amount of technical discussion can explain the curious believability of Beckmann's strange world. "Reality," he has written, "is the greatest mystery of our imagination. If you want to experience the invisible, devote yourself entirely to the visible." The statement negates the surrealists' method of approaching the intangible and the unknown, yet Beckmann, no less than they, arrives at a reappraisal of appearances which our minds may at first deny, but which our senses acclaim. To his exploration of reality, Beckmann brings a fierce strength and pride. He alone, as I said at the beginning, continues to prove the validity of the German expressionist uprising which occurred some forty-odd years ago.

TWO PAINTERS OF TRAGEDY: ROUAULT AND SOUTINE

Among painters of our century, two of the greatest masters of tragedy have been the Frenchman, Georges Rouault and the Lithuanian, Chaim Soutine. In them the troubled vision of Vincent van Gogh has found eloquent continuation, though neither painter has ever recognized their common spiritual progenitor with enthusiasm or even cordiality. Their affinity to van Gogh is in any case primarily the broad one of psychological malaise. On the other hand, these two twentieth-century painters have partaken of a specific, joint inheritance. Both have been disciples of those disparate masters, Rembrandt and Cézanne. For most contemporary artists, the example of the mature Cézanne has been an inspiration to refute the dramatic chiaroscuro of Rembrandt, to eschew open emotion and the outer expression of grief in favor of Cézanne's formal structure and daylight mood. But in the art of Rouault and Soutine, Rembrandt has reappeared, as if his were a humanitarian conscience come to qualify the brilliant discoveries of the post-impressionists, reminding us that emotional violence has often flared brightest in the Northern wind.

It is the curious amalgam of Rembrandt and Cézanne, then, which has given us these two great tragic painters: Rouault, a Celt and a Catholic; Soutine, a Baltic Jew. The two have spoken different yet universal languages, and their somber art has satisfied a deep contemporary longing for the spiritual content that modern painting has so often lacked or to which it has only indirectly confessed. The works of Rouault and Soutine have afforded penance to the frivolous, confirmation to the solemn and the sincere. The two artists have given us everything of anguish there is within them, and in so doing have provided a bitter but invaluable foil to the sensual relish and architectural purity so predominant, alternately, in twentieth-century art as a whole.

It would be difficult to find two painters less similar in background and temperament. The heritage of Soutine was one of Slavic melancholy, rough peasant vigor, almost barbaric appetite for visual luxury. Rouault's, on the contrary, is Northern Gothic, ascetic, scholastically rich; even the Byzantine aspects of his art spring more often from Rome than from the Near East which fed the Baltic's gaudy orientalism of brocade, metal and costume. His painting, though no less passionate than Soutine's, is more urbane, controlled and disciplined by myth, more knowing; and it is relieved at times by a humor totally absent from the latter's dogged and sorrowful pursuit of splendor.

The artists were born a full generation apart, Rouault in 1871 and Soutine in 1894. Their childhoods were vastly different. Rouault was born during the bombardment of Paris by the *versaillais,* his mother having taken refuge in a cellar from the terror of shells exploding nearby. No one can say accurately what effect birth under such circumstances might have on a child, but we do know that Rouault's youth was otherwise outwardly

Georges ROUAULT: The Old Clown, 1917. *Oil, 44¼ x 29⅜″. Collection Edward G. Robinson, Hollywood.*

undramatic. He grew up in a family of artisans. His father was employed in the Pleyel piano factory as a specialist in wood graining and finishing. His maternal grandfather, Alexandre Champdavoine, was a collector of Daumier lithographs who worshipped Callot, Rembrandt, Courbet and Manet, and fervently hoped his grandson would become an artist. As a boy, Rouault was encouraged to draw; he has described himself as a child sketching chalk heads in his grandfather's apartment, while the old clown, Grock, looked on and inquired gruffly why the heads should be larger than in nature. We know little about Rouault's relations with his father and mother beyond what is inferred by his own statement that his grandfather Champdavoine was his "sole spiritual support until Gustave Moreau." But he is said to have adored his mother, and he grew up in modest yet comfortable surroundings, in an atmosphere of rather special devotion to the arts and crafts. At fourteen, he was sent to the workshop of the stained glass maker, Hirsch, as an apprentice, with family encouragement and hopes for his future.

At fourteen, Soutine arrived in Vilna to begin two years of study at the Academy of Fine Arts. He left behind him in his birthplace, the ghetto at Smilovitchi, a childhood of unrelieved horror and physical pain. The son of an impoverished tailor, he had been beaten constantly by his father, who was particularly enraged by the child's absorption in drawing. On one occasion, according to Waldemar George's monograph on the artist, the youth stole some family household articles, sold them, and with the proceeds bought colored crayons. His father discovered the theft, and after beating him unmercifully, locked him in the cellar. After several days Soutine escaped and took refuge in the woods, where his mother fed him secretly.

The boy was expelled from school and once, if the legend may be believed, the entire village hunted him down in the forest, enraged by his habit of scratching images on the ghetto walls. He found shelter with the village simpleton and drew the man's portrait in gratitude. But even this touching gesture was not to go unpunished. When, slightly later, he was asked to draw the portrait of a local Rabbi, he arrived at the house only to be assailed by the Rabbi's sons, who called him a painter of idiots, presuming now to paint their father. He was so badly beaten that he was sent to a hospital, and relief came when his mother was able to frighten these or other assailants into bribing the boy not to complain to the dreaded Czarist police. With this money Soutine paid his way to Vilna; it was money earned by a youthful suffering as frightful as the most impassioned nineteenth-century Russian novelist could have devised.

We have from these accounts two very different motivations in childhood memory for the distraught visions which Rouault and Soutine were to express as adults. From the evidence at hand, it would appear that Rouault's childhood played no dominant part in the evolution of his tragic art, while Soutine's youth was clearly of overwhelmingly direct importance for his. We do not know what inner anguish Rouault felt as a child; we do know that he was capable of assuming sorrow imaginatively, so that the bits of Gothic glass he repaired in Hirsch's studio formed the Passion of Christ and his own as well. Moreover, Rouault's father, irritated by certain Catholic precepts of education, sent his son to Protestant schools for a time, and may have precipitated the spiritual conflict from which Rouault emerged a devout Catholic and the greatest religious painter of our time. And when, around 1903, he found his own voice, he used it to express a universal grief, absorbed as religious experience and projected again in terms of symbolic compassion. Soutine's painting, on the other hand, fed steadily on the personal memory of physical pain; its psychological root was a need for counter-violence.

Their careers begun, the two artists developed under almost opposite circumstances. Rouault's art was prepared by long formal training, first at the *Ecole Nationale des Arts Décoratifs* and, beginning in 1891, at the *Ecole des Beaux-Arts,* where he became a favorite pupil of Gustave Moreau, guided, supervised and encouraged over a long period of years. Soon after Moreau's death in 1898, Rouault was named Director of the *Musée Gustave Moreau.* It was a post which assured the young artist steady financial support, and it might well have committed him to carrying on the Moreau tradition of pre-Raphaelite sentiment, exotic sumptuousness of detail and a tried technique based on the sixteenth-century Venetians and Rembrandt. Instead, between 1903 and 1905, Rouault plunged into his own dark waters, as if he had tripped on a loose plank in the polished Moreau platform. He survived to take his place in the vanguard of the expressionist movement which the German artists of *Die Brücke* and the French *fauves* were then founding. From the beginning of his career he has lived a life of secrecy, meditation and esthetic research, protected by his curatorial position and seldom communicating with other artists.

In contrast to Rouault's life of economic tranquility, scholasticism and loneliness, Soutine's early years in Paris were ragged, starved and gregarious. Shortly after his arrival in 1911, he enrolled in the Cormon Studio at the *Ecole des Beaux-Arts,* paying his tuition with funds supplied by a doctor who had befriended him at Vilna. His classroom training was short compared to Rouault's, and if at Cormon's he came to venerate his lifelong idols, Tintoretto, Rembrandt and Courbet, it seems likely that he learned most from the artist-friends he soon made — Modigliani, Chagall, Kisling and others. He lived in an atmosphere of Bohemian give-and-take from which Rouault in his museum was completely removed.

For a time Soutine shared a room with Modigliani, whose knowledge of Cézanne, African sculpture and *avant-garde* tendencies in Parisian art must have been decisive in forming Soutine's anti-academic tastes. Soutine's friendship with Chagall may have been equally significant. During the years of the First World War, Chagall's works were widely published in such German periodicals as *Der Sturm,* and Chagall in turn was well informed about Central European expressionism. Through Chagall, Soutine could have known the works of Kokoschka and the artists of *Die Brücke* and *Der Blaue Reiter.* In any case the often repeated statement that he was himself a contributing force to German expressionism is clearly false, since his own expressionist style is much later in date. Whether by coincidence or not, certain of Soutine's earlier landscapes are close in spirit to Schmidt-Rottluff's fevered compositions of c. 1907. They utilize a frenzied technique — what the Germans derisively called *Schmiermalerei* — which made a modern reappearance in the art of late nineteenth-century German artists such as Lovis Corinth.

Rouault and Soutine, as was natural considering their respective ages, attained full power at different periods. From 1905 to 1918 Rouault produced the magnificent paintings of prostitutes, clowns (page 93), judges and Christs which have earned him rank as one of the major artists of our century. These pictures were followed by the incomparable etchings for *Miserere et Guerre,* by a full decade of printmaking to the partial exclusion of easel painting. Over the past fifteen years he has held his solitary eminence, gaining in skill and serenity, becoming more painterly, and sacrificing in the process some of the tremendous force of his earlier works.

Soutine's mature career did not begin until toward the end of the First World War. From roughly 1918 to his death in 1944 he produced the painting by which he is internationally and unmistakably known, an art of slashing impasto, free emotional distortion and what Alfred Barr has called a "strung and scrambled richness of pigment." At Céret in the Pyrenees and later at Cagnes, Soutine developed a full tumult of personal idiom in those dizzily arranged landscapes which seemed to the critic, Elie Faure, as if painted "in the course of an earthquake" (opposite). The landscapes were followed by still lifes of dead animals and interspersed with the portraiture to which his esteem for Modigliani may originally have led him. Nature, death and the riddle of the human face — these were his themes, restricted in manner and content, but made distinguished by Soutine's rending vertigo and bursts of color.

Rouault has been only slightly less limited in iconographical range, and both artists found their strength in a kind of mortal combat with the medium, rather than in an extension of its ideological or compositional possibilities. Between them they exemplify a philosophy which has reached a climax of application in twentieth-century painting, though often foreshadowed in earlier Western art and a recurrent earmark of Eastern: the funneling of inspiration to a narrow container of meaning. Whereas the portraitists of the eighteenth century had often disputed among themselves as to whether the eyes or the mouth should provide the sharpest point of interest in their images, there is no apportionment of intensity in paintings by Rouault and Soutine. One feels, in fact, that their relatively simple subjects were chosen for their capacity to convey an even heat; their impact is over-all and deliberately condensed. "I can look at the knot in a piece of wood till it frightens me!" William Blake once exclaimed. Soutine's art indicates a comparable squinting in the interests of ultimate realization, while Rouault's apocalyptic visions ascend a constricted path. It was perhaps because post-medieval Western art furnished them so infrequent an example of blunt and innocent emotion, that the two painters turned often to less circumlocutory sources: Soutine to African tribal sculpture; Rouault to Coptic fabrics, Byzantine mosaics, Persian miniatures and twelfth-century Gothic glass windows.

In technical procedure the two artists differed widely. Rouault, as we know, has often

Chaim SOUTINE: The Old Mill, Near Cagnes, c. 1928. *Oil, 26 x 32½". The Valentine Gallery, New York.*

worked on the same canvas over a period of five, ten or even twenty years, sometimes retouching it almost steadily, sometimes holding it in wait for the final enrichment of a day's elation or a year's distress. He has painted thinly in wash; he has piled layer on layer of pigment; he has used an unconventional technique of oil, watercolor, gouache, pastel and crayon, in unpredictable combinations. Since the First World War his inspiration has been fairly constant and unfluctuating, a steady interior illumination, so that he has felt free to treat his art as a whole, bringing sections of it to completion at one time, others at another.

Soutine's method was quite opposite. His medium was oil, simply. Like the majority of modern artists he carried each picture through to completion under the sway of a self-contained and temporal compulsion: if the final result pleased him, the picture was preserved; if not, at once destroyed. While Rouault for all his technical eccentricity has worked with something of an alchemist's slow method, Soutine attacked his canvases like a madman. "And he makes his canvas suffer, and the colours, the world of his suffering," Drieu La Rochelle has written. "Around him his tubes and brushes, emptied and smashed, strew the ground."

Soutine was dependent on reality as a point of departure to a degree that Rouault was not. For if Rouault during the early years of his career transformed actual visual experiences into ferocious images of moral judgment, as in the series of Versailles prostitutes and Parisian lawyers, he later worked from imagination alone. Soutine, however, consistently worked from the model. He needed a tangible focal point, a physical presence, to sharpen his concentration and fury. He took great pains to find the *right* model, and Michel Georges-Michel describes his living like an animal in a country stable, rising at three in the morning to walk twenty kilometers in search of a suitable subject for a landscape, coming back to fall asleep supperless on a bed of straw.

A more dramatic illustration of Soutine's need for objective stimulus is provided by the oft-told story of the side of beef. Soutine bought the huge carcass from a butcher and hung it in his studio during warm weather. The meat decomposed rapidly, and in its putrefaction the painter found more and more to engross him, new jeweled colors appearing in the rotting flesh. He worked with fanatical zeal, resting his eyes occasionally by painting the hands of a girl who sometimes posed for him. Finally his labors were interrupted by the sanitation officials, who came on complaint of the neighbors to demand that the stinking, fly-covered carcass be removed. Soutine argued bitterly, and was especially incensed by a compromise suggestion that veterinarians inject the beef with chemicals to halt further decay. As to the flies, he protested, "The Little One [his model] chases them, and then I can see those marvelous colors."

At intervals, so the legend goes, Soutine freshened the side of beef by spattering it with blood. How far we are here from Rouault, in whose imagination the blood from the Crown of Thorns is fresh and unfading! Nor can we imagine Rouault resting his eyes in the physical sense by painting white hands instead of red beef. For if Soutine depended on his eyes as channels to a tormented inner consciousness, Rouault has been a mystic who once wrote: "Subjective artists are one-eyed, but objective artists are blind." The two artists by different roads arrived at an extraordinarily eloquent expression of tragedy: the one often concerned with the tempers, anxieties and eventual disintegration of the flesh; the other preoccupied with a transcendental vision of man's moral indignities and the fate to which, eventually, he departs the earth. And while Rouault's unshakable faith has earned him a serene old age, Soutine's tragic death at forty-nine symbolized, in a sense, the more earthy and physical torment of his art. On an August day in 1944, he lay in a Paris hospital and Dr. Grasset the younger sewed up again as horrendous a still life as Soutine had ever created — the hopelessly ulcerated stomach which had fed on and in turn nourished the despair that made him so fine an artist and so tragic a human being.

THREE HUMORISTS: KLEE, MIRO, CALDER

Perhaps one day among twentieth-century art's many distinctions will be counted the rediscovery of visual wit as a relatively independent species of humor. The sculptors of the Middle Ages who created gargoyles as a relief from the tensions of faith, occasional draftsmen of the Renaissance and the Baroque, tribal craftsmen averting their own heady fears, the Daumier who noted Louis Philippe's resemblance to a pear — these and innumerable other artists through the ages understood that humor can be a matter of visual notation purely. But many more artists have been illustrators of a humor which either stemmed from verbal descriptions or could be conveyed equally well in words. We think at once of the Dutch and Flemish masters for whom drinking, vomiting and urination were so appealing a theme; of the later satirists who borrowed from the theatre such comic personages as The Ailing Female, The Miser and The Hypochondriac; of the genre painters of the nineteenth century, so tiresomely devoted to homely, long-winded anecdotes. In our own century, however, a few important artists have brought humor again within the fairly separate range of plastic expression, and among these Klee, Miro and Calder are outstanding.

All three artists have assigned the written word to a role of intensifying accessory instead of dominant source. No one, of course, can deny the importance of the title, *Twittering Machine,* for the Klee here reproduced (page 100). The image is laughable to begin with, but to enjoy it fully we must know what manner of machine is shown. Yet once the subject is identified, visual expression takes over completely, and what is portrayed is not a literary idea but an auditory experience, as often happens in Klee's art. And note with what extraordinary subtlety the sound of the image is conveyed. The bird with an exclamation point in its mouth represents the twitter's full volume; the one with an arrow in its beak symbolizes an accompanying shrillness — a horizontal thrust of piercing song. Since a characteristic of chirping birds is that their racket resumes as soon as it seems to be ending, the bird in the center droops with lolling tongue, while another begins to falter in song; both birds will come up again full blast as soon as the machine's crank is turned. The aural impression of thin, persistent sound is heightened by Klee's wiry drawing, and his color plays a contributory part, forming an atmospheric amphitheatre which sustains and amplifies the monotonous twitter.

The title of the Miro reproduced is more elaborate. It is called *Persons Magnetized by the Stars Walking on the Music of a Furrowed Landscape* (page 101). The title is not used in this case for purposes of identification only, but also to provide a poetic, verbal accompaniment, in the proto-surrealist manner founded by Marcel Duchamp, Max Ernst and Giorgio de Chirico. But the humor is primarily visual with auditory overtones, as it is in the Klee, and if the words add to our enjoyment of the image, they do not de-

Paul KLEE: Twittering Machine, 1922. *Watercolor and ink, 16¼ x 12". The Museum of Modern Art, New York.*

termine the picture's content. It is helpful to know what causes the strange behavior of Miro's three figures, but we need not know this to appreciate their giddy form. The creature at the left has surrendered to a celestial magnetism, and is floating lumpily upward, in helpless apprehension. The one at the right, its neck grievously stretched, clings to the musical earth with a fearful effort, suggested by the dotted, trembling contours of its body. The central figure is an agitated witness of his companions' enchantment, and appears to be protected from a similar fate by a cloud of light color above its head which insulates it from the pull of the stars. Yet even when we have deciphered or invented this much of a scenario for Miro's painting, we do not particularly keep the

Joan MIRO: Persons Magnetized by the Stars Walking on the Music
of a Furrowed Landscape, 1939. *Oil, 18 x 13⅛". Collection Mr. and
Mrs. H. Gates Lloyd, Haverford, Pennsylvania.*

story in mind. The main impact of the image comes from an autonomous caricatural
energy and from a precise balance of biomorphic forms.

Alexander Calder prefers the terse, descriptive titles used by Klee (and by Miro customarily, except in the latter's very recent works). Calder's *Cockatoo* (page 102) may be
admired as one of his most inventive sculptures even before we know its name. Yet in
this instance the identifying label is perhaps more closely related to the inception of the
image than is the case with either Klee's painting or Miro's. We cannot say for certain,
nor can the artist himself, whether the memory of a cockatoo inspired Calder to recreate
its appearance in abstract terms, or whether he completed his mobile and was then struck

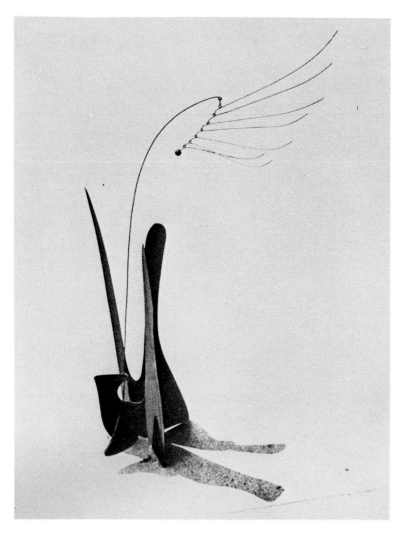

Alexander CALDER: Cockatoo, 1941. *Sheet steel and wire, 36¼" high.*
Collection Mr. and Mrs. Earle Miller, Downington, Pennsylvania.

by its resemblance to an exotic bird. It seems more likely, however, that the former sequence is true. Far more than Klee or Miro, Calder depends on an uncanny sense of
observation to generate his sculptured forms, especially when these forms refer to animals, birds and fish, as they very often do. (It may be argued in fact that his American
vision is matter-of-fact, in the literal sense of the phrase, by comparison with Klee's
Germanic cabalism or Miro's Catalan fantasy.) In any case, our pleasure in Calder's image is greatly increased by our recognition therein of the cockatoo's vain, nervous cockade, its counterbalanced tail and chunky body. Nevertheless, the image is overwhelmingly visual in conception, and if we did not know its explicit references, we

would still respond to the gaiety of its fluttering wires, the appealing flamboyance of its heavy base.

If all three artists are among modern art's finest humorists — and they are, of course, much more than that — there are important differences in the quality of their wit. Of the three, only Klee was mystic in the intensity of his laughter. In a previous book on Klee's prints, I referred to his "spirituality of humor," and I can now find no other term to describe the ethereal nature of his perception. It is true that many of his pictures are based on specific incidents or observed natural phenomena, so that he never lost contact with reality altogether. But his vision was transcendental, and he achieved in the end an almost religious profundity of humor. Deeply musical, he seemed to translate optical sensation into another language, communicating with the very core of our consciousness. He was assuredly the greatest, incomparably the most varied, visual humorist of our time, and his own brilliant accomplishment is described in a quotation from Gogol which Klee included in his diary for 1904: "There is a laughter which is to be put on the same dignified level as higher lyrical emotions, and which is as distant as heaven from the convulsions of a vulgar clown."

By comparison with Klee, both Miro and Calder are earthy in humor. The art of both abounds in sexual references which are altogether physical in nature. Both men, indeed, show a simple, animal pleasure in the physiological aspects of life, a directness of response to natural forms which contrasts with Klee's immense cultivation of spirit. Their art is less meditated than Klee's and narrower in emotional scope, but within its limits it is extraordinarily fresh and vigorous; it has a carrying power and heartiness to which Klee did not aspire. Both men have proved time and again that abstract art can be a vehicle for rare humor, and it was in part their historical function to break away from the deadly seriousness of the cubists and of later artists like Mondrian, and to restore playfulness and comedy to the repertory of abstraction. In so doing, however, they have sacrificed nothing but austerity; their humorous works are as inventive in the formal sense as those which they have completed in a more solemn vein.

Klee, Miro and Calder — what era can boast three comparable humorists who have been at the same time among the foremost stylistic innovators of their time? With them, at last, humor re-establishes its place in the fine arts, the eminent place to which these three artists and their precursors in earlier centuries have richly entitled it

ITALY: TWO MOVEMENTS, TWO PAINTINGS

It is the custom in this country to speak slightingly of modern Italian painting and sculpture as a national accomplishment. Indeed, the Italian contribution to the art of our period is seldom discussed as an entity, and there has never been an attempt here to exhibit it comprehensively, though various displays of an official or conservative nature have been held. This is a curious fact, but there are adequate reasons for it. To begin with, our nationalism of thought in art matters has focused on the American tradition, while Paris and Central Europe have between them exhausted our enthusiasm for foreign schools. Secondly, modern Italy has not produced many artists of international rank. It has produced, I think, one great painter, Giorgio de Chirico, and one important sculptor, Umberto Boccioni. It has produced a number of lesser figures of varying stature: Modigliani, Carrà, Balla, Morandi, Soffici, Severini, Fini, Campigli, De Pisis, Russolo and others. But some of these artists have been identified with Paris rather than Italy, while others have earned only local fame. And finally, it may well be that Italy's contribution to modern art was most persuasive during the decade of 1910–20, a considerable time ago.

However good our reasons may be, we are scarcely justified in consistently ignoring Italy's part, as such, in the art of our century. For Italy has given us two formal movements of decided esthetic interest: both have been unmistakably Italian; both have been attended by international repercussions in the visual arts, and without them the history of contemporary painting and sculpture would be poorer by far. It is the limited purpose of this chapter to describe the two movements briefly and then to contrast them through a comparison of two works by their leading proponents. The larger task remains, and it is to be hoped that there will soon be in this country a full-scale exhibition of twentieth-century Italian art, with an accompanying publication.

The first of the movements to be considered is, of course, futurism. Its very name has passed into our working language, becoming a rather unsteady signpost to those extremes of art and conduct which are more acceptable to the public if they can be identified romantically with the future. To many people futurism means simply the World of Tomorrow, an era in whose products a certain streamlined madness may now be pridefully expected; a futurist future with which our heirs must cope, but the result, nonetheless, of our own ingenuity. The word "futuristic" has become for the public one of the most inaccurate and comforting words in our esthetic terminology.

Perhaps this is all the more reason why futurism should be described again, however redundantly, in the terms of its original program and intention. The movement was launched in Paris on February 20, 1909, by Marinetti's manifesto in *Figaro*. It was a literary and political movement to begin with, but unlike surrealism, which experienced some initial difficulty in fitting art to its premise, futurism almost at once attracted five Italian painters — Boccioni, Carrà, Russolo, Balla and Severini. These painters, under Boccioni's direction, drew up their own manifesto in 1910 and expanded it by numerous subsequent declarations of faith, of which the most important is Boccioni's summary of futurist art, *Pittura Scultura Futuriste*.

The premise of the movement was relatively simple, though its esthetic platform grew complicated as time went on. Politically, futurism partly foretold the disastrous struggle to establish Italy as a great modern power; it was the nationalist trickle which swelled into Mussolini's fantasy, *mare nostrum*. It glorified war and proclaimed that only through militarism could Italy and her artists regain the vigor necessary to assure them world place.

The futurists recognized that war was an activity of young men, and they made much of their own youth. In his first manifesto Marinetti declared that all the futurists were under thirty years of age. When they reached forty, he added, younger artists would track them down in the countryside, and finding them "cowering" by their "trepidating aeroplanes," would put them promptly, though respectfully, to death. There was, however, a special penalty attached to youth in Italy: it involved the men in a concupiscence that the futurists condemned with Puritan fervor. A ruthless anti-feminism played an important part in the futurist creed. "We demand the total suppression for ten years of the nude in painting!" the painters exclaimed in their 1910 manifesto. It was their practical conclusion to a general tirade outlining the disastrous effect of women on art.

In woman's place as muse and object of adoration, the futurists substituted the machine. Their descriptions of the beauties of machinery were unrelievedly lyric, and it is interesting to note that their passion passed unabated to the second generation of futurist artists who made their appearance in the early 1920's. On January 11, 1923, Enrico Prampolini, Ivo Pannaggi and Vinicio Paladini issued a manifesto in Rome entitled "Mechanical Art." In it they wrote: "The beautiful machines have surrounded us and lean amorously over us, and we, instinctive savages and discoverers of every mystery, let ourselves be caught up in their frenetic whirl! Madly in love with machines, we have possessed them virilely and voluptuously." The language of the original futurists had been equally fervent. And Boccioni, one of the most ambitious artists our century has produced, extended the all-important inspirational role of machinery by suggesting that it should supply the actual ingredients of art. His list of suitable sculptor's materials, published in his "Technical Manifesto of Futurist Sculpture" on April 11, 1912, included: "glass, wood, cardboard, cement, concrete, horsehair, leather, fabric, mirrors, electric lamps, etc."

The futurist artists proposed to apply the shock treatment as a cure for the psychological illnesses from which Italian art had suffered since the death in 1770 of its last great master, Giovanni Battista Tiepolo. The injection to be given was contemporaneity, in fantastic strength. In our own country we have sometimes given the arts the same treatment, though only in mild and infrequent doses. But then, perhaps this is right-

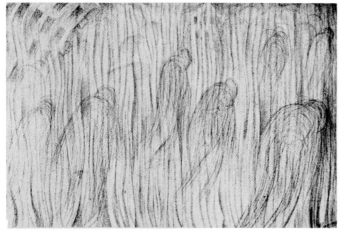

Umberto Boccioni: States of Mind, I, II and III (The Farewells, Those Who Stay, Those Who Go). *Pencil, each 23 x 34". The Museum of Modern Art, New York. Gift of Vico Baer.*

Umberto BOCCIONI: States of Mind, I: The Farewells, 1911. *Oil. Private collection, Italy.*

fully America's century, so that when our painters find inspiration in industrialism and the bright appearance of modernity, we think it natural if sometimes exaggerated. The early twentieth-century painters and sculptors of Italy, on the other hand, were living in the shadow of a great tradition, the greatest and most prolific in the world. They could not go anywhere in their country without being reminded of a past supremacy in the arts. Moreover, they were conscious of a debilitation of blood among their immediate forebears — those Italian artists of the nineteenth century who sometimes achieved a national prominence but never spoke with authority to the outposts of the world. The reviving force of the futurists was to be the brisk atmosphere of modern industrial life, breathed deeply. It did not matter that the air of Italy was in this respect rather thin; indeed, the vigor of futurism came in large part from the intensity of its wishful thinking, from its assumption of a partially hallucinatory talent for technology, from its degree of removal from the energy-centers of industrialism in America, Germany, and the England which as early as 1844 had inspired Turner's *Rain, Steam, and Speed.*

In order to apotheosize the present, the futurists first felt it necessary to repudiate the past. Thus Boccioni, the movement's most eloquent esthetician and foremost artist, described Raphael as "disgusting," Michelangelo as "disgraceful," the art of the Renaissance as a hindrance to modern creative activity. Yet the futurists, for all their invective against native tradition, could not conceal an underlying pride in Italy's accomplishment.

107

The violent patriotism which formed the core of their political philosophy, impelled them to defend the superiority of past Italian art to that of other nations. Without apparent realization of the paradox involved, they cited the greatness of their cultural heritage as proof that its continuation in futurism was to lead the way for living artists of other countries.

In publicizing themselves as the vanguard of contemporary art, the futurists were naturally troubled most by France's position as the established leader of advanced trends. Their writings about French painting revealed a psychosis peculiar to debtors. They admitted how much they had owed to impressionism, post-impressionism and cubism, but they claimed to have repaid the sum in full and at a very high rate of interest.

Their argument is forcefully given in the catalog for their Paris exhibition of 1912, signed by the five futurist painters. Here and elsewhere they praised impressionism for taking into account an interrelation of objects within a given scene, brought about by reflections of light. The impressionists, they felt, had broken down the traditional conception of subject matter as an assembly of fixed and fundamentally separate components. Further, the impressionists had noted the metamorphosis undergone by even the most solid and immovable objects due to the varying action of light, at different hours of the day.

According to the futurists, the impressionists had failed to carry their discoveries to a logical conclusion, for not only light passed from object to object, it was claimed; the forms of the objects were in themselves inter-reactive. The futurist painters pointed out in their manifesto that this was in certain instances a physical fact — "Our bodies sink into the sofa upon which we are seated and the sofa penetrates our bodies." It was also a psychological necessity, they asserted, that the artist be free to modify the external appearance of objects through subjective emotion based on memory, experience, and state of mind. In their own case, this emotion was to be expressed in terms of a rhythmic flow of moving forms; its wellspring was to be speed. They considered that the impressionists had unduly limited themselves in keeping separate records, by stages, of the object's metamorphosis under changing light. Why not run together in a single image a series of impressions? Why not an art of multiple exposure within a given frame? They called the principle for which they argued "simultaneity"; it became one of the cardinal points of their esthetic creed.

The futurists credited the post-impressionists, especially Cézanne, with having gone beyond the surface manipulation of the impressionists and with having restored solidity of structure to painting, paving the way for the cubists. They hailed the cubists' accomplishments in breaking down the artist's dependence on external reality. The cubists, they said, had evolved a "pure painting" of independent identity and validity. But the futurists' own program was to be more thoroughly anti-humanist than that of the cubists, who so consistently used the human figure as a point of departure. It was the five futurist painters, not Picasso or Braque, who wrote: "Our altered consciousness will no longer allow us to consider man as the center of universal life. The suffering of a man is of the same interest to us as the suffering of an electric lamp which, with spasmodic starts, shrieks out the most heart-rending expressions of color."

The futurists' praise of the cubists was liberally mixed with blame. They declared that Picasso, Braque, and their followers had frozen the imagery of a non-objectivity; in restoring solidity to painting, they had anchored their analytical elements so firmly that their volumes did not budge or interact and were presented in relatively static cross section. The reform proposed by the futurists was "dynamism." They defined the term elaborately, but at bottom it meant simply an imaginative setting in motion of external reality, under the direction of the artist's inspiration. The futurists described inspiration as an "inborn gift for complementarism" — as good a way as any of saying that only a born painter could paint a picture, particularly a futurist picture.

Futurism was essentially a crossbreeding of impressionism with cubism: motion from one and form from the other. The futurists, above all Severini, often retained the brilliant coloring of the impressionists and the post-impressionists, and it seems likely that they were directly criticizing the restrained palette of the cubists when they wrote: " . . . it will quickly be apparent that brownish tones have never circulated under our skin, that our flesh glows with yellow and flames with red, and that green, blue and violet flicker over it with a thousand beguiling graces." The futurists' brilliant colors were sometimes used not only for structural and decorative reasons, but as emotive equivalents for sounds and smells, it being their ambition to extend the sensory range of the painted canvas by appealing to the ear and nose as well as to the eye. The colors were applied in richly diverse forms indicative of motion — directional lines and planes, interpenetrating cubes and spheres, torpedo-wakes of color, blurred and overlapping contours, sweeping arabesques and vibrating prisms. Perhaps futurism's greatest accomplishment was in founding a vocabulary of such forms which later artists drew upon freely and which was everywhere vulgarized by commercial devotees of the romantic cult for streamlining.

Today, after long cross-examination under time's glaring light, the claims of the futurists seem exaggerated, especially as to originality. Their attacks on cubism are weakened by the fact that they appear to have misread or only partially read the cubists' pictures. The principle of "simultaneity," for example, is now known to have been implicit in Picasso's cubist works of 1909–10, most conspicuously in certain heads presented as seen from different viewpoints, at varying moments of time. Furthermore, the pre-futurist planes of both Picasso and Braque frequently denote a shifting motion, as if the volumes were not entirely fixed. This motion is, of course, merely *suggested,* and here we come upon a restricting fallacy of the futurists' own premise as applied to esthetics. Theirs was a premise which in a sense pre-empted for the artist the function of audience as well as of creator. "From now on," the futurist painters wrote, "we will place the spectator at the center of the painting" — another way of saying that they did not intend to allow him a separate existence. The futurists therefore tended to incorporate the observer's reaction within the picture. They often made motion so unmistakable that it ceased to be motion at all, except within the isolated confines of a given composition. And since painting is an art of communication more than of exposition, nothing now seems more static and self-exhausting than many futurist pictures, while the early works of the cubists stir with increasing life.

There are notable exceptions to this statement. Boccioni's monumental sculpture, *Unique Forms of Continuity in Space,* is a convincing, revolutionary, and deeply moving work of art, which not even several million senselessly imitative automobile fenders have been able to spoil. Balla's famous *Dog on a Leash* trots with believable and engaging alacrity, and there are canvases by Russolo, Severini, Carrà and, above all, Boccioni that continue to hold our attention. Yet the futurists failed to produce a major artist, unless Boccioni may be considered one, and perhaps the most successful single futurist painting is the *Nude Descending the Staircase* by the non-futurist, Marcel Duchamp.

The behavior of the futurists deserves separate comment, and has been of extreme importance for the history of modern esthetics. As is now well recognized, it was the anti-art demonstrations of the futurists that set the pattern for later dadaist and surrealist activities of the kind. Moreover, the futurists' protestations against the hallowed past and the sluggish present were conceived with a grandeur which has not yet been rivaled. It must be remembered that the antics of the dadaists and the surrealists were usually witnessed by limited gatherings; the *bourgeoisie* was slapped in small numbers. Most of the dadaist-surrealist fervor was expended in cafés, rented halls, and other places of assembly whose capacity was countable. Even on this scale, the model of chaos was established by the futurists. It was impossible for later groups to outdo their plans for theatrical *divertissements* which included orchestra seats covered with glue and, on the stage, the most haphazard and garbled admixtures of unrelated scripts and sounds. The technique was founded once and for all, and survives in the American stage productions of Olsen and Johnson. Its formula was to involve spectator and actor in unpredictable and noisy lunacy, with liberal aid from such practical devices as sneezing powders, explosions and other dependable irritants to the nerves.

The futurists have never been surpassed in planning large-scale demonstrations. Azari, known as "The Futurist Aviator," published in 1919 his plans for an aerial theatre in which innumerable planes, camouflaged by the futurist painters, were to execute futurist poems in the air, to the accompaniment of the utmost din their exhaust pipes could be made to produce. His plan was never executed, but the futurists did involve entire cities in their activities. They declared that Florence, Venice and Rome stank with art, reaction and tourists; and in the second-named city alone rained down 800,000 leaflets from the Clock Tower of the Piazza San Marco, denouncing to the populace its retardative life on the banks of a sewer.

The futurists were able to reach such large audiences because their program, in absolute contrast to that of the dadaists, was patriotic and nationalistic. They were vehemently pro-Allied, so that during the period between the outbreak of war and Italy's entry, huge crowds forgave or ignored their esthetic premise in a general sympathy for their

Giorgio de CHIRICO: The Melancholy of Departure (Gare Montparnasse), 1914. *Oil, 55 x 72". Private collection.*

political stand. But it must be added that the futurists paid unflinchingly for their nationalistic prestige. Nearly all of them showed exceptional conviction and courage in carrying their enthusiasm into action. Most of them fought with distinction in the war, and to it Boccioni gave his life.

Pittura metafisica was an almost absolute repudiation of everything futurism had stood for. Giorgio de Chirico put the matter unmistakably in an article for *Valori Plastici* significantly entitled "The Return to Craftsmanship." "On the other hand futurism," he wrote, "is a sort of confused d'Annunzianism and contains the same deficiencies and falsehoods: lack of depth; no sense of humanity; poor construction; hermaphroditism of sentiment; pederastic plasticity; false interpretation of history; fake lyricism. So far as artistic and technical integrity are concerned, futurism gave Italian painting the *coup de grâce*. Even before futurism it was wallowing in murky waters, but futurist excesses made the cup overflow."

Unlike futurism, with its fiery declamations and organized group activities, *pittura metafisica* represented a comparatively quiescent state of mind common to a very few artists. Its founder was unquestionably de Chirico, its only true convert during its few years of formal program, was Carlo Carrà. Carrà had been one of the five original futurist painters, but finding himself in love with Giotto and hence rather conspicuously disqualified for futurist attitudinizing against Italian tradition, had turned in 1915 to a primitivism of style based on the Assisi frescoes. Late that year or early in 1916 he became friendly with de Chirico, whom the war had brought home to Italy. The two men are said to have been rejected for military service on the grounds of mental or nervous instability — in itself, if true, a most significant indication of their temperamental opposition to futurism, with its unswerving militarism.

The two painters lived during the period 1916–18 in Ferrara, and for part of the time at least they were apparently detained by the military authorities, so that the art they evolved was quite naturally based on meditation as opposed to action. The fact of their sojourn in Ferrara is in itself relevant to their program. For whereas the futurists had shouted their contempt for Florence, Venice, Rome and other cultural centers, the two principal artists of the *scuola metafisica* developed their thesis in a town whose heritage was of a very special nature. Perhaps more than any other city in Italy, Ferrara is dominated by fantasy and by the tangible evidence of a restless dreaming, centuries old. The red architecture of the Castello Estense, which appears in several of de Chirico's 1916 paintings, the streets with their russet reflections and weird variety of buildings and ornamental detail — provided a peculiarly appropriate setting for the development of *pittura metafisica*. Ferrarese painting, too, is highly idiosyncratic, and there can be little doubt that de Chirico and Carrà were inspired by the magnificent frescoes of Cossa in the Schifanoia Palace, by the pictures of Baldassare d'Este, Ercole de' Roberti and Dosso Dossi, whom de Chirico later called an "apparitional" painter. It was in Ferrara, where the ape is so persistent an iconographical motif, that the mannequin, already utilized by de Chirico in his Paris works, assumed a new complexity and elegance and became a recurrent element in *pittura metafisica*.

De Chirico and Carrà remained the only consistent members of the *scuola metafisica*, though Giorgio Morandi and Ardengo Soffici experimented briefly with its style. (As in the case of futurism, a revivalist group appeared in the very early 1920's, including de Chirico's brother, Alberto Savinio.) The aims of the *scuola* were in essence a rationalization of the kind of painting which de Chirico had produced in Paris between 1911 and 1915, as noted briefly at the beginning of this chapter. But it was Carrà who first described the school's creed in print. His book, *"Pittura Metafisica"* (Florence, 1919), was bitterly attacked by de Chirico soon after its appearance; the association between the two artists ended, and with it the *scuola* as a cohesive movement. Nevertheless, the school carried along of its own momentum for several years, and was widely publicized from 1919 to 1921 by exhibitions and by Mario Broglio's magazine, *Valori Plastici*.

It was apparently Carrà's paintings rather than de Chirico's which exerted the stronger influence on a few Italian artists and on such divergent foreign painters as George

Grosz and the young Salvador Dali. For it is a curious paradox of art history that paintings may temporarily seem early if they were done only slightly late. Carrà's pictures, though they followed de Chirico's by several years, may well have appeared newer and more Italian to those Europeans outside France who associated de Chirico with the pre-war epoch of Guillaume Apollinaire in Paris. Moreover, Carrà's paintings probably transplanted better as illustrations of the "metaphysical" premise. They were school pieces in a sense that de Chirico's works transcended, and being this, were naturally more popular and more widely imitated. And finally, Carrà spoke with the authority of a convert from the spectacular philosophy of futurism.

The completeness of Carrà's about-face in renouncing futurism for *pittura metafisica* may be seen by comparing the two movements. To begin with, the basic conflict between them sprang from opposing attitudes toward native tradition. For the futurists, as has appeared, tradition had served mainly as an irritant, as both impediment and spur to progress. The painters of the *scuola metafisica,* contrarily, attempted to revive the arts of antiquity and the Renaissance by dreaming them into a new existence. Their paintings made frequent use of art objects as iconographical ingredients. While Marinetti had flatly declared that a speeding automobile was more beautiful than the *Winged Victory of Samothrace,* de Chirico used the Vatican statue of Ariadne as a persistent motif in his paintings of 1912–15. The futurist architect Sant' Elia condemned all past architecture and proposed that it be replaced by a functionalist skyscraper style. But de Chirico's early paintings are a nostalgic and extraordinarily poetic wake in memory of Italy's architectural past; the deep *horizontals* of Renaissance building are drastically exaggerated in his compositions and form the wings to a dream stage. The only machine which appears in de Chirico's early paintings, as I have pointed out elsewhere,* is the machine in the form of a man, that is, the mannequin.

The futurists had proposed a kinetic relationship between objects shown in their paintings; the artists of the *scuola metafisica* froze their objects in a staring immobility, as if viewed in a moment of hushed suspense. The dynamism of the futurists was replaced in *pittura metafisica* by a revival of the fifteenth century's fixed linear perspective, so that to the spastic motion of the futurists' works there succeeded an uncanny calm, peopled by the pointedly inanimate — statues and vegetables, mannequins and vans without wheels. Finally, to the futurist principle of simultaneity the *scuola* opposed a program of static incongruity. They did not attempt to synthesize different viewpoints and states of emotion in a whirling whole, nor to revitalize an existing visual order through the factor of imaginative motion. Instead, they stressed the fragmentary illogic of objects separate and clear, each with its identity preserved, each with an apparitional vitality of its own heightened by its dissimilarity to the others. For the physical and nervous interrelations of the futurists they substituted two amalgamating agents: traditional pictorial composition; and metaphysical acceptance of a counter-reality based on reverie. "I paint what I see with my eyes closed," de Chirico said, which was a very

* *The Early Chirico,* Dodd, Mead & Co., New York, 1941.

113

different matter from painting what the futurists saw through their wide-awake, cinematographic vision.

The almost total differences between the two movements may be understood by comparing two paintings of railroad stations, the one by de Chirico (page 111) the other by Boccioni (pages 106 and 107). Boccioni's picture was one of a series of three "states-of-mind" paintings which he included in the futurist exhibition of 1912 under the titles *The Farewells, Those Who Stay* and *Those Who Go.* (It seems curious that he should have chosen a railroad station for his locale instead of an airport or a garage, though it should be remembered that futurist art was more colored by sentiment than its apologists would admit.) Boccioni charged his scene with the dynamism of a new age; he made the laggardly Italian trains run *ahead* of time, so to speak. De Chirico, on the other hand, converted the *Gare Montparnasse* in Paris into an emotional replica of a Renaissance *piazza.* He turned time backward rather than forward. His inspiration was based on nostalgia for the Italy he had left, while Boccioni's sprang from an eager anticipation of an Americanized future. And whereas Boccioni's canvas is concerned with the passage of time and with recording simultaneously its fleeting seconds, de Chirico's painting stops time at the precise hour shown unmistakably on the station clock. For the heady rush of progress, de Chirico substitutes the fixed moment of omen.

The protagonists of Boccioni's scene are restless human beings embroiled in the futurist passion for speed and travel. But in de Chirico's picture nothing moves except the station pennants flying in a ghostly breeze. His train pauses to emit a cotton-puff of smoke; the station is inhabited by bananas, huddled as in sleep, and by two diminutive phantoms whose long shadows anchor them to a ramp so steep as to make motion impossible or at least extraordinarily difficult.

The kinetic energy of Boccioni's composition explodes in all directions, but de Chirico's scene is an absolutely quiet labyrinth, curtained at the left, blocked at the right, and admitting no easy egress. De Chirico's painting, indeed, revives the "thoughtful immobility, ecstasy and sleep" which Marinetti in his first manifesto had declared that futurism intended to replace with "aggressive movement, feverish insomnia . . . the slap in the face, the punch with a fist." The reaction had come full cycle.

A comparison between Boccioni and de Chirico serves to point up a chronic conflict between the present and the past as sources of inspiration for modern Italian artists. According to recent accounts, the conflict appears to have continued during the Second World War, with Giorgio Morandi occupying a middle position not unlike that which André Derain held for so long in France. At the one extreme Léonor Fini is said to have become the most spectacular defender of tradition's capacity for inventive reinterpretation, basing her art on the more fantastic aspects of sixteenth, seventeenth, and eighteenth-century Italian painting. At the other extreme the futurists have been replaced by the social realists as champions of a relatively self-sufficient contemporaneity. We must wait to see whether nostalgia or revolution will be the prevailing force for the younger artists of Italy whose names, after five years of war, we now begin to hear.

WYNDHAM LEWIS' VORTICISM

On June 20, 1914, the first number of *Blast* appeared in London, its magenta covers proclaiming its title in such exclamatory type that even now the magazine, if carried unwrapped through the streets, attracts startled glances from passersby. *Blast*'s editor was Wyndham Lewis, its sub-title, "Review of the Great English Vortex." Its temper was belligerent and wildly confident: "so England," it proclaimed, "is just now the most favorable country for the appearance of a great art." Today in England vorticism is seldom mentioned, and Wyndham Lewis lives in obscurity, many of his paintings having disappeared mysteriously. Yet it seems to me likely that he will rise again in his countrymen's esteem, and it is an interesting fact that his influence may be felt now in the work of two exciting young Scotch artists, Robert Colquhoun and Robert Mac-Bryde (pages 148 and 150), while an outstanding painter of the slightly older generation, Edward Burra, owes him much (page 144).

I cannot for one thing understand how Lewis' historical position may be ignored, for it was with his vorticism that a truly "modern" English painting was announced. Describing the movement twenty-five years later in *Wyndham Lewis the Artist,* its inaugurator proudly claimed that vorticism had constituted for the first time in English history a pictorial activity strictly contemporary with that of the Continent. This, however, was a slight exaggeration, since cubism and futurism predated the English movement by six and four years respectively. Still, it would be difficult to overemphasize the importance of vorticism, which served eventually to overthrow the absolute domination of the Bloomsbury group, with its basic addiction to the hedonistic, decorative standards of late nineteenth-century art. Yet vorticism was itself part of a general reaction against impressionism which made itself felt in London following the large exhibition, "Manet and the Post-Impressionists," held at the Grafton Galleries in 1910 and directed by the arch prophet of Bloomsbury, Roger Fry.

That exhibition had created an uproar and attracted a large audience. Women, half indignant and half proud, had proffered the art of their children as superior to that of Cézanne and Matisse; a Dr. Hyslop had lectured on the exhibition's contents as supplying clinical evidence on the meanderings of the insane; the newspapers had printed innumerable letters of assault and protest. (This public bile was regurgitated, astonishingly unaltered, on the occasion of the Picasso-Matisse and Klee exhibitions held in London during the winter of 1945–46. The press was equally violent, the public no less puzzled; the daughter of Holman Hunt maintained the tradition of invective in proper form by rising in a lecture hall to denounce Picasso's pictures as "vile garbage masquerading as art . . . the work of a diseased mind.") But however deep the reactionary animus against it, the Grafton Galleries exhibition of 1910 inspired a wave of revolutionary excitement among artists of advanced inclination in London. Within a year or two,

Frank Rutter informs us in his *Evolution in Modern Art,* "London had painters as 'wild' as any in Paris."

A number of these artists followed the expressionist lead of van Gogh (and later of Matisse), whose subjectivity of approach seemed in potential harmony with what Robin Ironside has described as "that minor lyrical tradition . . . that has been kept flickering in England ever since the end of the eighteenth century, sometimes with a wild, always with an uneasy light, by a succession of gifted eccentrics. . . ." Yet there were a few painters and sculptors in London who interested themselves in the more objective and architectonic goal indicated by Cézanne and the cubists. The most talented of these men grouped themselves around Wyndham Lewis and helped him with the publication of *Blast,* to which the First World War put an end after two issues. The central literary figure in the vorticist uprising was Ezra Pound; the most active painters were Lewis, Edward Wadsworth, William P. Roberts, Frederick Etchells and Cuthbert Hamilton; Gaudier-Brzeska was the group's leading sculptor, while Jacob Epstein was informally involved in its activities.

But what did *Blast* propose, and what was the premise of vorticism? In the first issue Pound declared: "The vortex is the point of maximum energy. It represents, in mechanics, the greatest efficiency." He added: "Every conception, every emotion presents itself to the vivid consciousness in some primary form." From these statements we may deduce several characteristics of the vorticist movement: its emphasis on peak force; its identification with machinery; its insistence on primary expression and mistrust of circumlocution in any of its numerous forms. But when we attempt to discover from vorticism's adherents what, more specifically, the movement proposed, we are forced to fall back on those strong negative statements which were a specialty of *Blast*'s editors.

The temper of the magazine, as briefly noted, was unrelentingly violent, and much of the text in the first issue is given over to ferocious attacks on futurism, as though it seemed crucial to knock Italy out of the running in art matters, leaving the field to France and England. Thus it was declared: "AUTOMOBILISM (Marinetteism) bores us. We don't want to go about making a hullabuloo about motor cars, anymore than about knives and forks, elephants or gaspipes. Elephants are VERY BIG. Motor cars go quickly. . . . The futurist is a sensational and sentimental mixture of the aesthete of 1890 and the realist of 1870." But having by inference disposed of the Italians as naïve and hopelesly flamboyant, *Blast*'s editors were apparently unable to formulate a positive counter-program. They continued to speak in negatives. "We do not want to change the appearance of the world," they said, "because we are not Naturalists, Impressionists or Futurists (the latest form of impressionism) and do not depend on the appearance of the world for our art." And having once more reproved the futurists for their effulgent manners, the vorticists concluded on a note of vague restraint: "Blast presents an art of individuals."

By July, 1915, when the second and final issue of *Blast* appeared, the horrors of war had tended to discredit futurism's exultant militarism and with it the movement itself.

Wyndham Lewis: Plan of War, 1914. *Oil. Whereabouts unknown.*

The futurists themselves were beginning to experience doubts; late in 1915 or early in 1916 Carlo Carra was to desert the movement for *pittura metafisica,* while before his death in 1916 the greatest of the futurist artists, Umberto Boccioni, repudiated the tenets he had once proclaimed so passionately. With this self-dissolution of futurism in the air, *Blast*'s editors softened their attacks, and even accepted in their pages the leading English futurist, C. R. W. Nevinson, who had returned from the trenches to denounce Marinetti and his followers. Cubism, however, remained a formidable rival of vorticism, and hence demanded a careful invective. While now giving qualified applause to the futurists' "vivacity and high-spirits" — qualities which only a year before had appeared so distasteful — Lewis declared: "The whole of the modern movement, then, is, we maintain, under a cloud. That cloud is the exquisite and accomplished, but discouraged, sentimental and inactive, personality of Picasso. We must disinculpate ourselves of Picasso at once."

In particular Lewis objected to the cubists' restricted iconography; he described as "an absurdity and sign of relaxed initiative" Picasso's absorption in still life and figures. He himself was an anti-humanist. At least he so appeared when he wrote in *Blast* "My soul has gone to live in my eyes, and like a bold young lady lolls in those sunny windows." But he was presumably reproaching Picasso not so much for his occasional concern with the human figure as for his neglect of what Lewis considered the greatest source of inspiration for contemporary artists — the machine.

In defining the kind of subject matter which they themselves proposed to explore, the vorticists as a group were torn between their contempt for the futurists' "Automobilism" and their own very real regard for the machine age in which they lived. Their jibes at Marinetti in the first issue of *Blast* are followed by the solemn declaration: "Machinery is the greatest earth medium: incidentally it sweeps away the doctrine of a narrow and pedantic Realism at one stroke." The vorticists in theory at least planned to depend on machinery as the initiator of new forms in art, and years later Lewis wrote: "the hard, the cold, the mechanical and the static . . . it was those attributes for which Vorticism had a particular partiality." He added: "Vorticism accepted the machine world: that is the point to stress. It sought out machine-forms. The pictures of the Vorticists were a sort of machines." To understand the revolutionary impact of such an esthetic for the London of 1914, we need only recall how consistently the rival Bloomsbury group proposed a warm, sensual, anti-mechanical and individualistic art.

But how did the vorticists differ from the futurists in their attitude toward our industrial civilization? The main difference clearly was that the vorticists planned to slow down and externalize the futurists' treatment of machinery. Thus if futurism may be described as impressionism set in motion, vorticism may be described as futurism brought to a halt, with liberal though unacknowledged aid from the braking power of cubism. "The [vorticist] artist," Lewis wrote in *Wyndham Lewis the Artist* (1939), "observed the *machine* from the outside. But he did not observe the machine *impressionistically;* he did not attempt to represent it in violent movement. For to represent a machine in violent movement is to arrive at a blur. . . ." He went on to say: "It [vorticism] did not sentimentalize machines, as did the Italians . . . it took them as a matter of course. . . . It was a stoic creed: it was not an uplift."

But though machine forms appear often in the early paintings of the vorticists, they are less dominant than the movement's manifestoes in *Blast* would lead one to expect. A number of the pictures reproduced in the first issue, for example, are not so much visions *of* machinery as visions experienced *from* a specific machine — the aeroplane.*

---

* Was there a philosophical as well as an esthetic basis for the vorticists' and futurists' faith in altitude as an aid to inspiration? If so, precedent is provided by the mid-nineteenth-century words of Baron Alexander von Humboldt, so important for romantic artists of the period: "In South America populous cities lie at an elevation of 14,000 feet above the level of the sea. . . . What may we not, therefore, expect from a picturesque study of nature, if . . . a feeling for art shall at length be awakened in those elevated regions." (Cf. Albert TenEyck Gardner, "Scientific Sources of the Full-Length Landscape — 1850," *Bulletin of the Metropolitan Museum of Art,* vol. IV, no. 2, Oct., 1945.)

Wyndham LEWIS: Women, c. 1921. *Oil. Whereabouts unknown.*

Edward Wadsworth's *A Short Flight,* Lewis' *Plan of War* (page 117) and *Timon of Athens* seem directly inspired by aerial topography, as the titles of the first two paintings would indicate. Their hard, geometric forms are related to those of Malevich's suprematism, founded in Moscow the previous year, but their reference to mood and inclusion of atmospheric values relates them strangely to certain "metaphysical" still lifes later executed by Giorgio de Chirico, notably *The War* (1915) and *The Revolt of the Sage* (1916). Etchell's prints of 1914 reflect an interest in topography similar to that of Lewis and Wadsworth, though his paintings are plainly cubist in derivation. And Roberts' *Dancers,* also reproduced in *Blast*'s first issue, makes clear that the futurist doctrine, however reviled, contributed importantly to the vorticist vocabulary.

The vorticists' faith in machinery as a unique source of form appears, however, to have been short-lived. Gaudier-Brzeska, at the time of his early death in the war, had planned to publish in the second issue of *Blast* an essay entitled "The Need of Organic Forms in Sculpture." The points he intended to make are summarized by Ezra Pound in his monograph on the sculptor. It was Gaudier-Brzeska's contention that machine forms were more suitable to painting than to sculpture, since the sculptor depends for effect on simplified mass, while the painter is free to combine a great variety of pictorial motifs. Moreover he believed that machinery itself had more or less exhausted its own esthetic potentialities in three-dimensional terms, whereas these potentialities were still open to two-dimensional reinterpretation by painters. There is evidence, however, that the vorticist painters were less and less inclined to accept machine forms as their chief and exclusive responsibility. By 1915 Lewis was writing in *Blast:* "But I think a great deal of effort will automatically flow back into more natural forms from the barriers of the abstract." He added: "Nature with its glosses, tinting and logical structures, is as efficient as any machine and more wonderful. . . ."

In these comments about nature and the machine, both Gaudier-Brzeska and Lewis were, of course, speaking about a relatively abstract art and its possible sources, not about strict likeness to an external model, whether natural or machine-made. Yet the problem of naturalistic representation engrossed the vorticists as an irritation of which they could not be entirely rid and to which Lewis was forced to give grudging recognition. "Only after passing a most severe and esoteric Board and getting a CERTIFICATE," he said in the second *Blast,* "should a man be allowed to represent in his work Human Beings, Animals or Trees."

The vorticists' difficulty in dismissing the problem of realism lay, of course, in the fact that it had been solved so brilliantly by artists of previous centuries. And unlike the futurists, the vorticists were able neither to bring themselves to take tradition lightly nor to revile it as a hindrance to modern creative activity. Though Lewis warned against too close a dependence on the Old Masters and described Michelangelo as "probably the worst spook in Europe," haunting British art without respite, the attitude of the vorticists toward the past was on the whole respectful. Ezra Pound was especially firm in his mistrust of the futurists' posturing against tradition. "It may be," he wrote in his book on Gaudier-Brzeska, "that Italy was so sick that no other medicine could avail, but for any man, not a modern Italian, to shirk comparison with the best work of the past is gross cowardice." And again referring directly to the futurists, he added: "The Vorticist has not this curious tic for destroying past glories."

The vorticists' regard for the past did not, however, prevent them from reappraising it in the light of their own predilections and activities. Their movement shared with cubism and Central European expressionism a strong liking for exotic and primitive cultures, a highly selective and critical attitude toward the arts of antiquity and the Renaissance. Both Epstein and Gaudier-Brzeska owed their main inspiration to the Egyptian, Assyrian and Polynesian sculptures in the British Museum, and Pound spoke for them when he wrote: "The Renaissance sought for a lost reality, a lost freedom. We seek for a lost reality and a lost intensity." Gaudier-Brzeska, for one, continually referred to the great classicists as "those damned Greeks," and quite evidently preferred the trans-Mediterranean art of more enigmatic civilizations. As for vorticism's unofficial associate, Jacob Epstein, his debt to the Egyptians is evident in his Oscar Wilde memorial of 1909–12; by 1912–13 he was capable of turning from the abstract style of his *Mother and Child, Two Doves* and carvings in flenite to the African primitivism of *Cursed Be The Day Wherein I Was Born.* Lewis at a later date in his career was profoundly influenced by the carved figures of New Ireland (page 119).

The vorticist movement, as already noted, was disbanded by the First World War and was never to be revived. Gaudier-Brzeska, infuriated by the German bombardment of Rheims, joined the French army and fell early in action. Epstein, whose *Rock Drill* of 1913 remains one of the most distinguished twentieth-century sculptures and summarizes much of the vorticist premise, turned to portraiture during the war. The new artists recruited by Lewis for the second issue of *Blast* were of minor consequence. William Roberts became an official war artist and afterwards turned to a Mannerist figure style abounding in wryly humorous distortions. Lewis himself went into the army. He had been one of the first artists in Europe to undertake pure abstractions, but after the war he reintroduced the human figure, either in compositions influenced by Oceanic sculpture or through a personal kind of cubist portraiture. By 1932 he was ready to declare: "I move with a familiarity natural to me amongst eyeless and hairless abstractions. But I am also interested in human beings." The vorticist revolution was over long since.

By comparison with cubism, futurism or even Russian suprematism, it had not been a particularly brilliant revolution. But it had attracted world attention to modern English art, and it had included in Lewis, Roberts, Wadsworth, Gaudier-Brzeska and Epstein figures of lasting interest. Perhaps most important of all, as noted briefly at the beginning of this chapter, it had overthrown the exclusive authority of what we think of, accurately or not, as the "Bloomsbury" esthetic, with its emphasis on sensibility and on decorative standards carried over from late nineteenth-century French art. Once vorticism had made its appearance, the way was clear for English artists already alert to the more advanced tendencies being explored on the Continent. It is scarcely an exaggeration to say that vorticism was a vital factor in the death of one century of English art and the birth of another — the twentieth.

STANLEY SPENCER

Mary Chamot in her *Modern Painting in England* generalized as follows about the English artists who gathered around Roger Fry before and after the First World War. "All their paintings," she wrote, "show a deliberate desire to suppress the very English tendency to elaborate detail." The statement is true of Duncan Grant, Vanessa Bell, Matthew Smith and many other artists born around 1880, who evolved an art of simplified communication based on late nineteenth and early twentieth-century French models. Even Paul Nash carried on in more advanced terms a paring away of ornament in favor of skeletal structure, and certain English abstractionists of the mid-1930's adopted such rigidly non-figurative standards that Myfawny Evans declared in their behalf: "A hair's breadth between two positions of a shape on a background makes the difference between one picture and another."

There is, however, an important English artist who in early maturity went counter to the prevailing tendency and chose instead to follow the abandoned and brambled path of the Pre-Raphaelites, though with very decided deviations. This artist is Stanley Spencer, and it seems strange that in England, where critics almost unanimously acclaim the eccentric gifts of Blake, Fuseli and Palmer, only divided attention is paid Spencer. Perhaps this is because he has stood apart from the contemporary movements: in reply to John Rothenstein's questions as to his views on advanced trends in French and English art, he once replied: "I can tell you no more than a charwoman could . . . I'm simply unable to understand modern painting."

Spencer was born in 1891 at Cookham on the Thames and grew up in an atmosphere of extreme piety and devotion to the arts, particularly to music. His forebears were villagers who, as often happens in England, had created for themselves a life of intense intellectual activity, out of the simplest means, in close devotion to each other, and with the Bible as the over-all authority in what was effectively a home university. Stanley's grandfather was passionately interested in astronomy and his father, inheriting the interest, was given an observatory by a nobleman of the vicinity whose wife later provided the funds for Stanley's art training at the Slade School. The father, a builder by trade, was also a professional musician, and had so thoroughly educated himself that he was able to tutor two of Stanley's brothers for their courses at Oxford and Cambridge. The eldest of these brothers was a child prodigy at music and afterwards professor at a leading German university; the entire family was erudite, talented — and simple.

Stanley, the seventh son among eleven children, went to school in Cookham where his own sisters were his teachers. At fourteen he was allowed to specialize in drawing, and illustrated fairy stories for the pleasure of the family. At sixteen he decided to concentrate on drawings of architecture, having been inspired by Edmund New's illustrations for the *Natural History of Selborne*. The choice was logical for a builder's son, and throughout his career Spencer has rendered architectural details with unusual devotion and sensitivity. In 1909, after a dreary year at the Windsor School of Art, he was sent to the Slade School of Art at University College, London, and remained for three years, to his vast pleasure and benefit. At the Slade he was undoubtedly exposed to the Italian primitives and to the great fifteenth-century masters whose influence may sometimes be detected in his own painting. Yet John Rothenstein wrote of him in 1927: "His interest in the art of painting as such has never been a great one. . . . He feels that inspiration carries within itself the power to fulfill it."

It would be difficult to imagine a less fashionable theory to have held in the era of Sickert's followers and Roger Fry, when English painters so consistently drove themselves to emulate the French facility with technique. Moreover, we know that Spencer was unfashionably excited by the competitions for original compositions on sacrosanct themes which the Slade assigned its students during their vacation periods. His brother Gilbert, Henry Lamb, Ethelbert White and Edna Clarke Hall were spiritual allies, at a slightly later date, in an attempt to revive the idealism of the Pre-Raphaelites, in opposition to the rising cult for egocentric and anti-iconographical expression. Of these associates perhaps the most important is Henry Lamb, a medical student turned artist, who came under Spencer's influence just before the First World War, though he had previously painted one of the most original and moving of modern British pictures — the *Death of a Bretonne* of 1910.

After leaving the Slade, Spencer returned to Cookham, and until the war the village was the main inspirational force in his work, as Shoreham had been for the youthful Samuel Palmer nearly a century earlier. Toward the end of his student days, his paintings had sometimes shown traces of Augustus John's penchant for broad masses and summary handling. But in *The Nativity* (1912), there appeared on the one hand a Pre-Raphaelite intricacy of detail, on the other a flat manipulation of form which seems related to that of Maurice Denis and other Parisian symbolists, though far less urbane, and marked by what R. H. Wilenski has called an "earnest dignity." The picture heralds a central preoccupation of Spencer — the translation of Biblical subjects into terms of Cookham's contemporary local color.

If *The Nativity* seems at casual glance to be dominated by the idyllic artifice of the Pre-Raphaelites, it is nevertheless replete with bold distortions which lead to the violent mannerisms of *The Apple Gatherers,* painted the same year. And in the *Zacharias and Elizabeth* of 1913, the figures assume an enigmatic intensity of expression and posture which takes Spencer away from the polite opulence of Rossetti toward the graver mysticism of Blake. The atmosphere now becomes visionary rather than decorative, the figures move as in a dream of ancient legend, the primitivism of approach seems compulsive rather than merely stylistic. In his *Visitation* (1913) there is an emphasis on psychological innuendo which his works as a student had never shown.

During the few years that remained before he joined the army, Spencer completed several paintings which are still among his most impressive, notably *The Resurrection of Good and Bad* (1914), *The Bed Picture* (1915) and *Swan Upping at Cookham* (1915). What strange and haunting pictures all three are! The first-named shows fantastic beings emerging from the ground: the good find themselves in a landscape of clear light and Pre-Raphaelite flowers; the bad wear slabs of the heavy earth, like restraining capes which they try to shake loose. The Resurrection was to become the dominant theme in Spencer's art, and the two panels of *The Resurrection of Good and Bad,* daring in format and composition, are surcharged with a pre-humanist intensity, incredulous, innocent and powerful. The "Resurrection of Bad" panel illustrates a recurrent compositional device in Spencer's art — the molding of inanimate objects to complement the human figure in outline and empathic relationship.

Once seen, even in reproduction, *The Bed Picture* is unforgettable. It portrays a square bed in an otherwise unfurnished room, with one child sprawled on the covers and three others kneeling in gloom and apprehension on the far side. The picture is usually interpreted as a depiction of children's fright at the news of war. Yet the fear exhibited seems hardly so tangible, as if it were inspired by childhood imaginings alien to the world of adult events. The children appear engrossed in that inner and separate life which the novelist, Richard Hughes, described so brilliantly in *A High Wind in Jamaica.*

Spencer's own childhood has affected his painting to an extraordinary degree, and certainly his psychology has been molded by the special circumstance of his youth as one of the youngest in so large a family. Furthermore, Elizabeth Rothenstein informs us in her monograph that the artist was unusually small as a child. She writes: "He was so tiny that no one could think he was beginning to grow up. Many of his pictures show this vision of things seen as a child sees. He remembered how queer things looked when observed from below . . . the oddity of a room seen through the bars of a cot . . . And he loved strange, almost distorted shapes, and remembered to incorporate them in paintings executed years later."

The most ambitious of Spencer's pre-war pictures was *Swan Upping at Cookham* (opposite) in which villagers carry trussed swans from the Thames to brand them with their owners' names. Here, as often in Spencer's art, a connection is established between humble incident and an implication of historic event, emphasized in this instance by ancient costumes traditionally worn for the ceremony. The figures in the foreground are simple Cookham workmen drying their boats. But directly behind them walks a *quattrocento* boatman who carries cushions elaborately upholstered in the Omega Workshop style, like a Magus bearing gifts. From a magnificently painted bridge in the background the proceedings are watched by an oracular figure, posed like one of the Furies. The composition is organized with a swelling power and through a weaving counterpoint of forms which recalls Spencer's self-avowed debt to music as a source of both inspiration and plastic structure. We have his own word for the fact that the composition of his master work, *The Resurrection of Soldiers* at Burghclere (1926–32) is based on the fugue. In youth he had had a vision of angels "shrieking with joy" when one of his

Stanley SPENCER: Swan Upping at Cookham, 1915. *Oil, 56 x 46". Collection J. L. Behrend, Burghclere, England.*

brothers had played Bach's *St. Anne Prelude and Fugue* on the village organ. Throughout his career he has consciously attempted to transpose music into visual forms.

Spencer served for four years in the First World War as a private, first as an orderly in Bristol War Hospital and then, for nearly three years, as an orderly and infantryman on the Macedonian front. Immediately after the war, in 1919, he was able to translate some of his recent experience into the large painting, *Travois Arriving with Wounded at a Dressing Station, Smol, Macedonia* (Imperial War Museum). A comparison between this picture and Henry Lamb's *Bombardment in the Judean Hills,* which also hangs in the Imperial War Museum, reveals how drastically Spencer stripped the Pre-Raphaelite vocabulary of its redundancy and clutter. Lamb's painting is executed with the tight prolixity of a Holman Hunt, each of its thousands of stones delineated with precision and care. Spencer's canvas, on the other hand, is organized through bold parallel forms which give it an immediate over-all impact. The comparison between the two pictures is especially revealing in that both are painted as if seen from a nearby raised viewpoint, with attendant use of foreshortening.

After the war Spencer returned to Cookham, and from 1919 to 1926 painted a series of landscapes whose straightforward and polished realism attests his pleasure at being home. But he was no longer a villager, and for a number of years Cookham was to play a less pervasive role in the inspiration of his truly imaginative works — his figure pieces. Macedonia now obsessed his thought, and memories of the Balkan campaigns constantly· swarmed to mind. At times, indeed, his art reflects a confusion of imagery between Cookham and Macedonia. Years after the war, for example, he tried to recapture the excitement of a childhood Christmas morning at Cookham, painting *The Nursery* (opposite). But the central figure of a kneeling boy is taken from his Burghclere mural of a resurrection of soldiers at Kalinova, Macedonia. The boy is arranging paper houses which recall the tents in a second Burghclere mural, *Camp at Kalinova.* Moreover, Spencer in a letter to Richard Carline once declared that *Camp at Kalinova* was deliberately composed so as to give the feeling of the scene's being within a house, a feeling "which Macedonia gave me in a place where there was no sign of it." We also know that Kalinova had so impressed Spencer when he saw it as an orderly that he asked for combat duty in order to return there. It therefore seems reasonable to suppose that he subconsciously identified Kalinova with his home at Cookham. For a long time after the war, images of the two places overlapped in his mind.

Whatever their exact psychological effect, Spencer's war experiences transformed him as an artist. He no longer worked as a naïve visionary, but as the inventor of distortions and iconographical fantasies; in his post-war figure painting he belongs to the tradition of Fuseli more nearly than to that of Blake or the early Palmer. Yet it must at once be added that if innocence and primitive wonder are gone from his works, their eccentricity still seems truly compulsive, rooted in an inescapable craving which has its way with him and often results in astonishingly forceful images. There is little sense of outright fabrication in his art of the 1920's, no use of shock value for its own perishable virtue, none of that bibliophilistic reference to fantasy in past art which has been so common lately in the works of the lesser surrealists. He remained original and creative; the impetus and variety of his imagination stand out as rare phenomena in twentieth-century English painting. His key works of the period are *The Last Supper* (1920), the Macedonian-inspired *Christ Carrying the Cross, The Betrayal* (1922) and above all *The Resurrection* (1923–36), Spencer's most famous picture, now in the Tate Gallery.

Stanley SPENCER: The Nursery, 1936. *Oil, 30⅛ x 36⅛". The Museum of Modern Art, New York.*

In 1923 Spencer completed a large pencil and wash cartoon and numerous other sketches for a series of mural paintings based on his memories of the war. On seeing the sketches Mr. and Mrs. Louis Behrend not only commissioned the artist to execute the murals but erected a chapel, the Oratory of All Souls and Almhouses at Burghclere, Berkshire, to contain them. In 1926 the artist began work, and the stupendous task occupied him until 1932. He made surprisingly few changes in applying his sketches to the walls, as may be seen by comparing the 1923 cartoon, published in R. H. Wilenski's 1924 monograph on the artist, with the detailed photographs of the completed murals reproduced in Elizabeth Rothenstein's recent book on Spencer. The murals cover three walls — the altar wall and two adjoining side walls. The altar wall is entirely filled by the huge *Resurrection of Soldiers,* while the side walls are divided into four arched panels, with predellas beneath and continuous murals above.

The subject of the chapel paintings divides into two general themes: incidents from his service as a hospital orderly; and scenes of an infantry encampment at Kalinova, Macedonia. All the side-wall panels are readily decipherable, and may easily be identified as pictures of soldiers camped in the field or performing their tasks as hospital orderlies. There does not appear to be a fixed plan of iconographical interrelation, though arched panels and predellas are arranged according to broad suitability of subject. Yet the panels, however readable, are far from being plainly realistic. All are subjectively transformed by the artist. The human gestures are Mannerist-Baroque in their tension and restlessness; the inanimate objects are acutely stylized and so disposed as to create a symbolic accoutrement for the figures.

Each section of the murals carries the mark of Spencer's devout response to a given incident of war. Thus the hospital gates are remembered because they had opened with difficulty and had assumed for him a religious significance. The soldiers in the upper section of *Drawing Water* appear like descending angels, though in reality they are reclining on a bank and reaching out their canteens to the flow of water. The incidents of menial servitude in hospitals are included because Spencer took pleasure in them, having read in the *Confessions of St. Augustine* a description of God as "fetching and carrying and coming and going." Viewed as a whole, the panels may be considered a humanist complement to Paul Nash's war paintings, in which nature is the protagonist. And for all their post-Raphaelite distortions, Spencer's murals sometimes recall the art of the mid-fifteenth century. Uccello in particular comes often to mind. Indeed, the foreshortened handling of the gear in *Stand-to* and the profile rendering of the mule in *Drawing Water* seem specifically related to Uccello's *Battle of San Romano* in the National Gallery, London.

The murals reach their climax in the altar wall's *Resurrection of Soldiers.* In the foreground section, deliberately planned so as to have an eye-level cohesion more or less independent of the upper action, soldiers emerge from the ground amid a sea of crosses, for which one of Lelio Orsi's sixteenth-century panels furnishes the closest precedent. Gradually the observer's eye ascends to the middle ground, where two white mules crane their necks in brilliantly opposed curves to see the diminutive figure of Christ in the upper ground. To Christ the soldiers in a contagion of faith are bringing their crosses, symbols of their demobilization at the end of their last earthly task. At Christ's right is a veritable ocean of mules whose massed grouping was inspired by a description in *Moby Dick* of a herd of whales so vast that it appeared to sailors like a bank of land. The wall as a whole is superbly balanced, each incident leading to another with sureness and conviction, each separately rich in interest and imaginative power. The chapel deserves to rank as one of the major achievements of twentieth-century English art.

During the 1930's Spencer's figure paintings grew steadily more distraught and mannered, while his landscapes and flower pieces, contrarily, became more literal than ever before. There is a crescendo of sexual torment in his works belonging to the first category, expressed on the one hand through a Freudian symbology, on the other through an open bestiality to which the art of certain German painters of the *Neue Sachlichkeit* furnishes the closest contemporary parallel. He was still able to paint occasionally in terms of simple village faith, as in *Sarah Tubb and the Heavenly Visitors,* which caused a considerable stir in the Carnegie International Exhibition of 1933 and was explained by the artist himself, in the *Carnegie Magazine,* simply as a record of a local religious incident. But his vision of Cookham was now often disturbed by nightmare transmutations and erotic savagery. His fantasy became vicious, haunted and bitter, notably in *The Dustman* (1934), *Sunflower and Dog Worship* (1937) and *Adoration of Old Men* (1937). In the mid-1930's he painted a *St. Francis and the Birds,* but a *Temptation of St. Anthony* might have reflected more accurately his own psychological state. (Ten years later he undertook the latter theme in a rather unsuccessful but psychologically revealing picture entered in the International Bel Ami Competition, held in 1946 by an American film producer.).

During the recent war, Spencer completed a series of paintings on the theme, "Christ in the Wilderness," and was commissioned by the War Artists Committee to paint a group of mural panels interpreting defense activity at the Clyde shipyards. He has also returned lately to his basic subject, the Resurrection, and has been at work in Scotland on paintings of contemporary figures redeemed from the earth. The paintings will eventually be composed into a series of triptychs.

Like so many modern artists, Spencer was a finer painter in youth than he has been recently. Yet his art of the past fifteen years is rich in invention, and its very fevers may one day give it rank only slightly below the pious works of his early career. Certainly there is no artist like him in the world today. He stands alone now, as he stood in youth. His solitary position may seem a greater virtue in future years, when the conformity of so much of twentieth-century painting may be more accurately appraised.

BEN NICHOLSON

Ben Nicholson, son of the artist Sir William Nicholson, was born in 1894 and studied art at the Slade School and in Tours and Milan. He completed his first painting in 1911, and from that year until 1919 he executed numerous realistic still lifes. Very briefly, from 1919 to 1920, he came under the influence of vorticism and painted portrait heads in the "mechanical" manner of Wyndham Lewis. His first truly abstract picture dates from 1923, and for the next ten years his work reflected the impact of various post-cubist developments in abstract art on the Continent. Picasso, Braque, Klee, Brancusi, Miro — these and other artists left their mark on his work of the decade 1923–33, and were it not for the change in his way of seeing which took place in 1933, he might be considered an extremely sensitive mirror to some of the greatest art produced in our time, though often highly personal in his reflection of the models before him.

There were, however, two constants in his long period of experimentation, and the change in his art, when it came, was a logical development of earlier tendencies. The first of these constants was his preoccupation with texture. Throughout the decade 1923–33 he explored innumerable methods of extending the range and variety of the picture surface, using heavy impasto, *collage* and then, in the early 1930's, applying plaster to the canvas and incising it to give his painting an engraved texture. Paul Nash, reviewing a Nicholson-Hepworth exhibition in 1932 declared: ". . . in the painting of Ben Nicholson, there is so much actual texture of surface that we are led to feel with our eyes, even if we can resist the temptation, as I could not, to stroke the hard and polished paint." Several years later, in describing an exhibition of Nicholson's more settled abstractions, Hugh Gordon Porteus observed: "Essentially [Nicholson's painting] is neither formal nor decorative, but tactile art . . . so much depends on texture — quality of paint, gesso, or board, direction of brush strokes, modulations of tone and surface — that the best photograph must be a travesty."

The second constant in Nicholson's period of preparation was his interest in deepening the spatial range of the two-dimensional canvas by the use of convoluted lines or carefully defined, superimposed planes. (The interest is, of course, closely allied to his preoccupation with texture.) Thus *Unit One* reproduced in 1934 a revealing photograph of his studio which shows two different bits of tapestry hung on the wall, one over the other, so that the contrasting patterns are thrown into relief. And we know from his own account in "Notes on Abstract Art," published in *Horizon,* October, 1941, that as he moved toward his ultimate solution of the space problem, he was haunted by the memory of a painting he had made in 1932 of a shop window in Dieppe. "The name of the shop," he writes, "was 'Au Chat Botté' . . . but what was important was that this name was printed in very lovely red lettering on the glass window — *giving one plane* — and in this window were reflections of what was behind me as I looked in — *giving a second plane* — while through the window objects on a table were performing a kind of

Ben NICHOLSON: Project, 1947. *Oil, 8¼ x 8⅜". The Lefevre Gallery, London.*

ballet and forming the 'eye' or life-point of the painting — *giving a third plane*. These three planes and all their subsidiary planes were interchangeable so that you could not tell which was real and which unreal, what was reflected and what unreflected, and this created, as I see now, some kind of space or an imaginative world in which one could live."

The painting, *Au Chat Botté,* represents the climax of his attempt to increase the number of planes in a given picture through traditional methods of color and line. Tentatively in 1933, definitively in 1934, he deepened the engraved or cut-out areas of his pictures, using thick wooden panels as a substitute base for plaster-coated canvas. He thereby arrived at an art of bas-relief in which the component forms were restricted to the square, the circle and the rectangle, and were excavated rather than built up.

Nicholson meanwhile had come under new and abiding influences — Malevich's suprematism, the abstract vernacular of *de Stijl* in Holland, Mondrian's later essays in exact proportion, the relief sculptures of Arp and of the constructivists, Gabo and Pevsner. For the benefit of those who are comforted by awkward labels, he might in fact be described as a suprematist-constructivist, at least in most of the works he has completed since 1933. But such a description would tend to minimize the real contribution that Nicholson has made to the art of our time. Arriving at a consistent style just twenty years after Malevich's first suprematist works and Tatlin's first relief objects, his part in compiling the dictionary of abstract expression quite naturally has been minor. But his virtues are his own, and I shall try to list some of them here.

To begin with, his three dimensional modulations of space are exceptionally subtle. While Tatlin, Gabo, Pevsner and Domela (though not Arp) in most cases had thrust out their relief forms boldly from the flat surface, Nicholson has held to the borderland between painting and sculpture. His incisions are seldom deep; they exist as the most delicate traps for light, which they can nevertheless absorb in such quantity that Herbert Read has remarked: "They are the only kind of painting that can look the sun in the face." Yet even strong side light does not turn his pictures into true sculpture; it only accentuates the vibrancy of their relationships, like a final tuning. The circles and rectangles of his 1933 pictures were often irregularly cut, with color overflowing the contours, and as late as 1935–36 he frequently used a bumpy over-all surface as an added beguilement for the eye. Lately, however, he has trued up his edges with mathematical precision (page 131), his surfaces have become more flat and uniform, and many of his paintings — the best of them — are almost entirely gray, white or buff, with only minor accents of strong color.

How is it that some of his most restrained and geometric abstractions have what may be described as an emotional tremble, in the good sense of the term? They show traces of the artist's devoted application; their surface is warm and alive. His pictures make no attempt to startle or please, and are uncompromising and crystal clear. Yet if the total difference in formal intent is kept in mind, they remind one of certain inspired English versions of French eighteenth-century Rococo, of those decorations in which a British reticence, longing and worship of material give this extraverted and alien style a new imaginative elegance. And as to decoration for its own sake, it would be difficult to think of a more suitable mural for a church than a large Nicholson panel. His few colors are saintly and tender; his quality is meditative and reverent. Further, the painter himself has written: " 'Painting' and 'religious experience' are the same thing. It is a question of the perpetual motion of a right idea." There is in many of his recent paintings an exceptional cleanliness, contrasting almost absolutely with that inspired negligence of which Miro is so consummate a master. Yet if Nicholson's art is never carelessly spilled, it is only occasionally cold or dry.

One source of its warmth it shares with a good part of recent English art, whether abstract or romantic or expressionist — its suggestion of historicity, its veneration for the fingerprints of time. Whereas the paintings of Léger and other Parisian abstract artists are often notable for their brash insistence on *newness,* the art of Nicholson, Hepworth, Moore and Sutherland frequently has overtones of an ageless past: in some of Nicholson's works the silence of Stonehenge, in a manner of speaking, replaces Mondrian's beloved Boogie Woogie as an offstage accompaniment.

Like many abstract paintings, Nicholson's pictures reproduce badly and appear monotonous. Moreover, some of them appear to be more completely school pieces in the

Ben NICHOLSON: Still Life, 1947. *Oil, 23 x 23". Collection F. L. S. Murray, London.*

manner of Mondrian than they actually are, though Mondrian's influence has clearly been of great importance for the English painter. But the best of Nicholson's works show notable differences in mood (page 131 and above). "A different painting, a different sculpture," the artist wrote in *Circle,* "are different experiences just as walking in a field or over a mountain are different experiences and it is only at the point at which a painting becomes an actual experience in the artist's life, more or less profound and more or less capable of universal application according to the artist's capacity to live, that it is capable of becoming a part, also, of the lives of other people and that it can take its place in the structure of the world, in everyday life."

Still, it must be admitted that Nicholson's paintings vary in quality. "We need not claim for them," Paul Nash once wrote, "that every one is a masterpiece; in an affair of such delicate nicety of direction and depth, the difference between something and nothing is an ace. The wastes of the desert or the Arctic floes are either worlds of infinite enchantment or they are wastes. Herein lies the adventure of this art."

GRAHAM SUTHERLAND

Of English painters who have come to international fame during the past five years, the most distinguished, I think, is Graham Sutherland. By earlier standards of truth-to-nature in art, Sutherland would certainly be considered an "abstract" painter. Yet he has always avowed his dependence on outer reality. In an interview by R. Myerscough-Walker, published in the English periodical *Artist* in 1944, Sutherland declared: "But broadly speaking, I should say that most of the objects which form my paintings I have actually seen in nature. I remove the traces of superficial reality or optical reality and try and retain the essence of the original object." And in explaining his own preoccupation with close-up rearrangements of natural forms, he added: "The aim of a painter such as we have been discussing [a painter such as himself] seems to me to be bound up with his ability to be able to select certain aspects of what he has seen and felt and, as it were, to caricature the *essence* or the *gesture* of reality." But nature is always the generating point of reference. Indeed, Sutherland is so confirmed a naturalist that to him may be applied Vasari's words on Piero di Cosimo: "He set himself often to observe such animals, plants and other things as Nature at times creates out of caprice, or by chance, in which he found a pleasure and satisfaction that drove him quite out of his mind with delight."

Sutherland was born in London in 1903, was educated at boarding school in Sutton and at Epsom College, worked briefly as an engineer and then, planning to become a painter, studied at Goldsmith's School of Art, London University, for six years. Together with his classmate, Paul Drury, and guided by the expert technician, F. L. Griggs, devout disciple of Samuel Palmer, he turned to etching and followed the line of descent in the graphic arts which includes Dürer, Rembrandt, Palmer and Edward Calvert.

Sutherland worked a good deal in the Palmer country of Kent, and over a period of years produced a series of etchings which are closely related to the prints of the "Ancients" — that early nineteenth-century brotherhood which gathered in the village of Shoreham and included the artists Palmer, Edward Calvert, F. O. Finch, George Richmond, Frederick Tatham, Welby Sherman, Henry Walter and the antiquarian, John Giles, all of them allied by their veneration for William Blake, their love of weather, their regard for the old architecture of England and for the pastoral Kentish landscape. Sutherland's early prints are in fact so dominated by the romanticism of the "Ancients" that they give little indication of the style he was later to adopt. He produced his etchings slowly, and most of them were post-card size or smaller, in deference to Palmer's faith in the "condensing power of art — a power which enables a painter to compress within a few square inches, as a poet does within a few lines, a universe of beauty and suggestion." They included a few Biblical figure subjects, but mostly they were landscapes in the Palmer manner. Exhibited at the Twenty-One Gallery in 1925 and 1928, they had a

Graham SUTHERLAND: Thorn Trees, 1945. *Oil, 42¾ x 39¾". The Albright Art Gallery, Buffalo.*

considerable success, and Sutherland might easily have settled down to a comfortable career as a modern "Ancient," secure in the by then widely accepted romantic tradition of Palmer and his associates.

He did precisely the opposite. Though he continued to teach printmaking, composition and book illustration at the Chelsea School of Art until 1939, his own last etchings were completed toward 1930. Among them is *Pastoral* which, as Edward Sackville-West has properly remarked, foretells the aggressive morphology of Sutherland's more recent works in gouache and oil. There followed a five-year period of slow experiment with painting during which the artist was often, and probably to his benefit, preoccupied with the problem of broad-scale design imposed by commissions for posters, fabrics and other decorative articles. In 1936, the year of the large London exhibition of surrealism, his painting was influenced briefly by that of the Parisian surrealists, notably Max Ernst, whose volume of prints, *Histoire Naturelle,* is allied in spirit to the subjective naturalism with which Sutherland was to replace the bucolic romanticism of his earlier career.

If the example of surrealism was a factor in Sutherland's decision to sharpen the psychological impact of his paintings, it is evident that in his art he has psychoanalyzed not himself nor his fellow man, but nature. In 1937 and 1938 he finished a number of paintings in which he first arrived at a settled conception. A few of these pictures are panoramic views; the best are close-up interpretations of natural forms, preserving these forms' basic identity, but removing them from their normal context by intense deformations of color and line. His basic vision established, Sutherland has since gained steadily in power and fluency, though he still uses oils more hesitantly than watercolor, chalk and gouache.

Between 1938 and 1940 Sutherland found his stride, painting *Gorse on Sea Wall, Association of Oaks* and *Green Tree Forms,* among other important works. He still lived in the tender countryside of Palmer's Kent, but he now went often, beginning in 1934, to the wild Pembrokeshire coast of Wales. "I wish I could give you some idea of the exultant strangeness of this place," he later wrote, "for strange it certainly is, many people I know hate it, and I cannot but admit that it possesses an element of disquiet." He added: "The whole setting is one of exuberance — of darkness and light — of decay and life. Rarely have I been conscious of the contrasting of these elements in so small a compass."

It was precisely this condensation of contrast which interested him most, and Pembrokeshire confirmed his belief that the fragment could be more revealing than the panorama, the "blow-up" of the section as evocative as the whole's reduction to minute, Palmeresque scale. He returned from his trips to Pembrokeshire with shells, roots and inexplicable stones, a stored imagery of ancient trees standing defiant and fierce on the blanched cliffs; and he brought with him innumerable careful drawings, some of which he worked up into paintings with only minor variations. Very often in his paintings, plants and trees assume an unmistakably human configuration, but his vision is opposite to that of Arthur Rackham, whose discursive fantasy of mind led him to convert

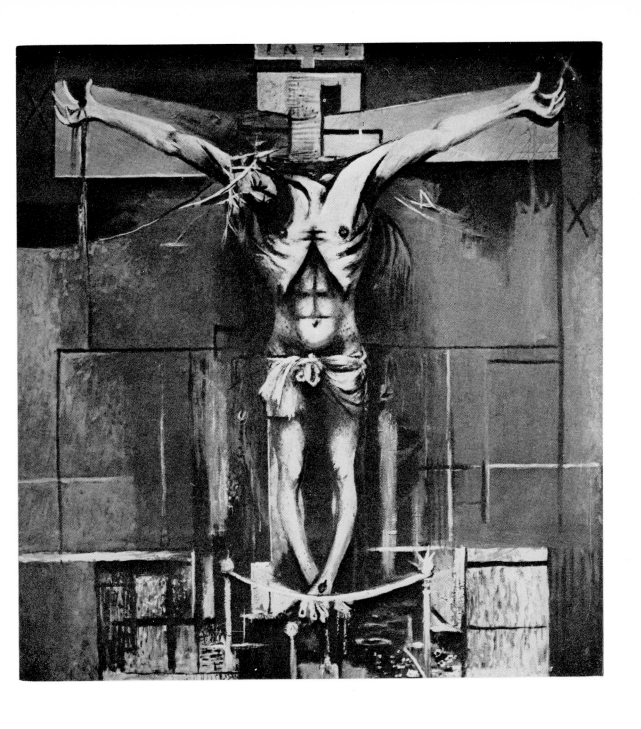

Graham SUTHERLAND: Crucifixion, 1946. *Oil, 8′ x 7′ 6″. Church of St. Matthew, Northampton, England.*

branches and twigs into a myriad of human visages. Sutherland sees nature as through a powerful telescope which takes images out of sequence and reveals them in a concentrated and ambiguous isolation. "In this area [Pembrokeshire]," he wrote, "I learned that landscape was not necessarily scenic, but that its parts have an individual figurative detachment."

If Pembrokeshire narrowed and toughened his way of seeing, his technical means simultaneously benefited from a study of the more advanced art of his own time. His chief debt since 1938 has been to Picasso (as he himself has acknowledged), particularly to the Picasso of 1932–37, and there is a decided kinship between the drawing in Sutherland's mature painting and the astonishing calligraphy of Picasso's *The Dream and Lie of Franco* and his sketches for *Guernica*. Yet Sutherland's color is his own — sulphurous dark green, rose and black, and that yellow-orange which recurs so frequently in English painting of the past five years.

Beginning in 1940 Sutherland was commissioned as an Official War Artist. He was least successful, it seems to me, in his early assignments, which included the documentation of ruined buildings in Wales and London and a few paintings of camouflaged airfields. His sympathy, as in the case of the late Paul Nash, is for nature, not for architecture or the machine. Moreover, he is at his best when he peers rather than scans. Thus among his most eloquent records of the war are those paintings in which a sense of unutterable havoc is conveyed by small, strewn fragments of reality — burned out paper lying on an East End pavement, a tortured oak, its roots exploded to the earth's surface and appearing like vengeful claws.

Sutherland himself is not satisfied with his war pictures, feeling that a certain realism was required and that there was not time to develop a suitable technique, particularly since some of the commissions were not sympathetic. Nevertheless, the finest of his wartime scenes complement Henry Moore's superb drawings and watercolors of tube shelters and mining scenes. (Sutherland appears to have done the latter subjects before Moore, though Edward Wadsworth had been a forerunner of both artists in his *Ladle Slag* of c. 1920, which had achieved a memorable abstraction of molten metal and light.) The sympathy between Moore and Sutherland is close and of long standing, and both artists have occasionally utilized a system of diminishing concentric perspective, first adopted by Moore in his tube shelter sketches of 1941. But Moore makes man the protagonist of all drama, while Sutherland customarily uses figures as accessories to nature or as points of reference for its forms. If we compare, for example, Moore's *Tube Shelter Perspective* with Sutherland's *Tin Miners — A Declivity*, the essential difference between the two artists becomes clear. In these two pictures the conception of perspective, the ceramic richness of color, the liberal use of ink accents — all are roughly similar. But Moore is concerned with slight shifts of posture in the reclining human figure, Sutherland with the soil's patina, the stains and clays of the under-earth.

Sutherland is a Catholic, and many of his paintings seem religious in fervor. We know, for example, that his recent preoccupation with thorn trees and bushes (page 135) sprang from his interest in painting a now-completed Crucifixion for the Church of St. Matthew in Northampton (page 137). Quite typically, he reduced his initial conception to minutiae which typified for him the point of sharpest psychological focus in the tremendous scene to be represented. He went to the core of drama, so to speak, and the many paintings he made of thorns prepared the portent of the Crucifixion itself. He did not, however, entirely surrender abstract form to expressionist emotion. In describing his ideological concern with thorns, he mentioned, too, his search for a biomorphic order — "A sort of 'pricking' and demarkation of a hollow headshaped space enclosed by the points." It was the head of Christ that eventually filled this space, but only after long, relatively formal experiment with contour and volume.

Today, in England, Sutherland is regarded by many competent critics as the outstanding painter of his generation. His progress toward a finished style has been slow; it does not show that early assurance which distinguishes the art of Georgia O'Keeffe, his nearest American equivalent in philosophy though not in technique. He has himself enumerated in *Signature* the subjective, native sources which have nourished him along the way: Blake's Dante drawings and wood engravings for Virgil's *First Eclogue;* Palmer's Shoreham watercolors and drawings; Turner's late paintings, such as the Tate Gallery's *Sunrise and the Sea Monster;* Paul Nash's paintings and his illustrations for Sir Thomas Browne's *Urne Buriall and the Garden of Cyrus,* described by Sutherland as "a poetic and imaginative achievement without equal today in this country"; and finally Moore's drawings of all periods.

Quite apart from the English sources listed in his *Signature* article of 1936, Sutherland has been inspired more recently by the Macedonian School of 1300, the late fourteenth-century School of Mistra, by Grünevald, Cranach, Seurat and Picasso. In a recent letter he remarked: "There has always been a certain duality in my likes which has presented the aim of investing one's invented symbols with physical presence and appearance." He adds: "As one grows older, of course, the things one likes vary. My aim is always to catch and pin down the essence of that aspect of reality which moves me — to fix and mark out the shape of my sensation."

What remains to be said, is that Sutherland has made of his sources an art of his own, compelling, strong, growing more impressive on longer acquaintance.

What is most impressive about English painting today is the number of good artists who emerged during the terrible years of the recent war. We cannot properly speak of these artists as constituting a "young" generation, since many are forty or over, but taken as a group they are remarkable in number, talent and range of approach.

If asked to name the most important single factor in the rise to a more international esteem of the new British school, I for one would mention the genius of Henry Moore. Lesser artists very often gain stature through the appearance of a giant in their midst, and Moore is widely recognized today as one of the half-dozen leading sculptors of our time. During the war, deprived of sculptors' materials, he became an astonishingly fine painter as well, though confining himself to small works in chalk, watercolor and ink. His shelter drawings (opposite) seem to me the most eloquent direct reflection of the war yet achieved by an artist, and I believe they already deserve rank with the drawings and watercolors of Blake and Palmer. Their influence in England has been immense. What is perhaps more important, however, is that their rare, humanist quality, together with that of Moore's sculpture, has focused attention on contemporary English art in general, and has given England's newer painters an assurance and daring they might not have shown without Moore's example. Since Moore is primarily a sculptor, he falls outside the range of this book. Yet he must be kept in mind, not only as the most distinguished of Britain's modern artists, but as a decided moral, inspirational and technical force among many of the painters who now begin to appear in important exhibitions.

The position of pure abstraction is less dominant in English art today than it was during the mid-1930's, which may well have been the climactic point of the abstract tendency in that country. Still, Ben Nicholson remains an impressive figure, and his wife, Barbara Hepworth, has grown steadily more original and sensitive as a sculptor and draftsman (page 142) ; her art is notable for an extraordinary purity. Arthur Jackson is a consistent disciple of the Nicholson-Hepworth interest in non-objective form, and lately abstraction has gained a talented recruit in John Tunnard, born 1900, who uses surrealism's far perspective as a backdrop to a close-up drama of abstract forms (page 143). Formerly a jazz band leader and a textile designer, he brings to painting a sense of asymmetric melody and a fine instinct for convoluted design, creating a romantic labyrinth in which abstract signposts are skillfully and unexpectedly disposed. Offsetting the gain of Tunnard, abstraction in England has lost perhaps its most inventive painter of the late 1930's — John Piper, who around 1938 began to abandon abstract art for a romantic, representational documentation of England's architectural treasures. The shift in recent English painting to what Piper himself describes as a "romantic revival," is nowhere more dramatically signalized than by a comparison between one of Piper's ab-

Henry MOORE: Two Sleeping Shelterers, 1941. *Chalk, watercolor, pen and ink, 15 x 22". Collection William Walton, London.*

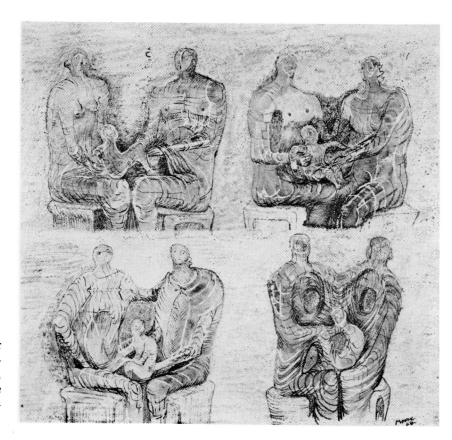

Henry MOORE: Studies for Family Group, 1944. *Watercolor, pen and ink, crayon, $18\frac{1}{8}$ x $18\frac{7}{8}$". Collection Miss Helen L. Resor, Greenwich, Connecticut.*

Barbara HEPWORTH: The Green Caves, 1946. *Gouache and pencil. The Lefevre Gallery, London.*

stractions and one of his later watercolors on an archeological theme (pages 146 and 147). During the long task of documentation to which the artist has devoted himself since 1940, he has evolved a fixed yet fluent style, in which Palmer's textural richness and Cotman's picturesqueness are combined with arbitrary use of chiaroscuro, sensitive drawing and a personal sense of color. Piper only occasionally falls into the abyss of romantic overstatement. And to those who object that in abandoning abstraction he has turned his back on his own era, the question may be put: which is likelier to be looked at with interest fifty years from now, Piper's abstractions or his documentary watercolors and drawings? The former, though real in quality, are not to be compared with those of the great Spanish and French abstractionists; the latter are almost unique in modern art in their eloquence as consecutive architectural records.

The brief and ecstatic enthusiasm for surrealism in England seems now to be largely spent or qualified in the direction either of dramatic satire, as with Edward Burra, or of lyric naturalism, as with the late Paul Nash, Graham Sutherland and numerous younger painters. Yet the revolutionary quality of surrealist art at its best still affects some at least of the more talented men. There is Ceri Richards (b. 1903), for example, who began his

John TUNNARD: Forecast, 1945. *Oil, 23 x 21½". Collection Sir David Scott, K.C.M.G., O.B.E., London.*

public career by exhibiting wooden bas-relief constructions which became progressively less abstract and more and more affected by the surrealism of Max Ernst. Just before the war, he developed a figure style based on Picasso's Baroque calligraphy of the late 1930's, and painted a series of coster-women notable for extreme boldness of line and color. He has perhaps not yet fought entirely clear of his sources, but he works with mounting assurance and a Welsh vigor of imagination. Lucien Freud has developed a naïve and occasionally touching poesy in which there are strong surrealist overtones; his drawings are sensitive, and at their best have the visual shock for which René Magritte's art has long been notable. And it remains to be said that the validity and importance of sur-

Edward BURRA: *Bal des Pendus, 1937. Watercolor, 62 x 43". Owned by the artist.*

144

realism have been defended in England lately by such men as Roland Penrose and Robert Melville, eloquently and well. These and other artists and writers have refused to surrender to a rising regard for the practical as opposed to the poetic and inspirational function of art.

There are in England today, as briefly noted, a number of artists devoted to dramatic fantasy, often with satirical overtones. Of these men Leslie Hurry and Michael Ayrton practice an art of imaginative elegance, affected by the tradition of "Gothick" melancholy; both seem primarily draftsmen and stage designers. The most prominent member of the group — its members are allied in broad spirit rather than fact — is Edward Burra, born in 1905 and trained at Chelsea Polytechnic and the Royal College of Art. His vision derives at bottom from Signorelli, the Spanish Mannerists and the Italian masters of the Baroque, but he has long since evolved a contemporary idiom of his own. His early drawings were influenced by Aubrey Beardsley in their macabre fantasy and use of ornament. As he has developed, the *art nouveau* predilections of his early career have been replaced by more vigorous sources — the early George Grosz (particularly in Burra's drawings), Picasso, Wyndham Lewis, Covarrubias, the early Miro and Dali. His paintings of the late 1920's and 1930's veered between a witty realism and a more arbitrary fantasy in which compositional procedure owed much to Continental experiments with *montage*. Despite ill health, he managed to travel extensively during the decade 1928–38, and his mordant sense of observation focused often on the gaudier restaurants, cafés and dives in New York's Harlem, the French Riviera, Mexico and Spain, so that for a long time he was chiefly notable for his hard, bright commentary on the seamier aspects of the contemporary scene — a Latin underworld counterpart to Evelyn Waugh's prose treatment of the vacuous pleasures of London's high Bohemia. Since the Spanish Civil War of 1937, Burra's art has become more somber and tragic, its fantasy concerned with evil and pain, its technique both more abstract and more feverish than ever before (opposite). Because of ill health, Burra works in watercolor, pasting together the sections of his large-scale compositions, but he now replaces the *montage* approach of his earlier years by a more cohesive use of linear perspective. From the beginning of his mature career, however, Burra has been able to assimilate his sources and to achieve a striking amalgam of Mannerist distortion with a still, metallic, almost vorticist treatment of detail acutely observed. In iconography he is among the most inventive of living English artists and technically one of the most skilled.

Whereas Burra's satire is related to external events and appearances, the art of Francis Bacon (b. 1910) is introspective, violent and motivated by a frightening psychological torment (page 151). There is no laughter in it, as with Burra in all save his recent works, but there is a strange obsessive force, an inner anguish, which relates it in mood to the painting of the young American expressionist, Hyman Bloom. Bacon's pictures, with their nameless terrors, contrast absolutely to a straightforward, dispassionate portrayal of one of mankind's most tangible catastrophes — *The Withdrawal from Dunkerque,* by Richard Eurich. They contrast as well with the graceful, mannered but accomplished

John PIPER: Forms on Dark Blue, 1936. *Oil, 36½ x 48½". Collection Mr. and Mrs. John Duncan Miller, Chicago.*

topographical art produced by many pupils of the Royal College of Art, among them Edward Bawden, Vivian Pitchforth and the late Eric Ravilious.

There is in England today a considerable group of younger artists, christened by one of them the "Euston Road School," and called by their enemies "The Fog Brigade," which re-explores impressionism and the atmospheric painting of the Sickert period. The group includes William Coldstream, Leonard Greaves, Anthony Devas, Lawrence Gowing and Victor Pasmore, among others. The last-named, born in 1908, seems by far the most talented, and it is possible that his quiet, sensitive painting will one day pass in esteem the more recognizably "modern" art of some of his contemporaries. In general premise the group is roughly related to the Parisian neo-romantic generation of 1926 — Bérard, Tchelitchew, Berman and Léonid — in that its members eschew ab-

146

straction and expressionism in favor of a caressing depiction of objects and figures deeply loved, conveying a mood of reverie and quiet appreciation. But whereas the Parisian artists took their point of departure from the early works of Picasso and de Chirico, the Euston Road painters have gone behind the entire School of Paris to rediscover Sickert, Wilson Steer, Degas and Pissarro (though at times, it must be admitted, Pasmore's earlier pictures remind us of Edouard Vuillard and Roger de la Fresnaye). The group as a whole runs the risk of merely repeating the formulas of the earlier "sensibility" school which grew up around Sickert, but certain of Pasmore's recent works appear to have achieved a moving lyricism of their own.

The war has intensified and brought to a head among younger English artists a return to native, romantic naturalism, with Blake and, above all, Samuel Palmer as special heroes of the new esthetic. For while the isolation of the recent war years if anything increased the interest of American painters in the art of a remote Paris, it naturally lessened British emulation of a France which, enemy held, was disastrously near. In any case, romantic naturalism seems now a dominant trend among younger English artists, though we must remember that Paul Nash was inspired by Palmer's giddy worship of

John PIPER: Lansdowne Crescent, Bath, 1942. *Watercolor, 15½ x 20¼". The Imperial War Museum, London.*

147

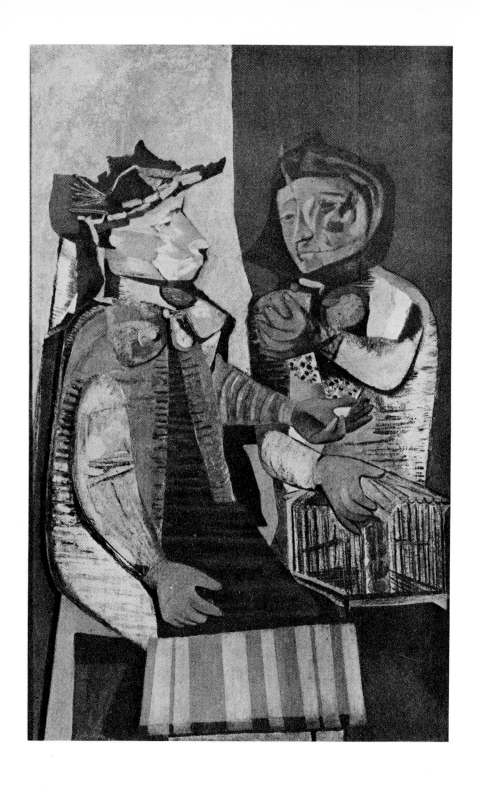

Robert Colquhoun: Women Talking, 1946. *Oil, 50 x 32". The Lefevre Gallery, London.*

148

nature as long ago as 1912, in a wash drawing entitled *Falling Stars,* while John Piper and Graham Sutherland have formed the taste of many of the newer men.

Sutherland's influence is paramount among younger artists working in the Palmeresque tradition, but often the latter combine his contours with Piper's lichened surface. John Minton, Keith Vaughan and John Craxton work very much in the Sutherland spirit, though with decided differences between them. Minton is the nearest to Palmer himself, Craxton closest to Sutherland in his use of condensed forms, while Vaughan combines the atmosphere and texture of Sutherland and Piper with a skilled, neo-romantic handling of representational figures. All three artists begin now to achieve more personal styles.

Two young Glasgow College graduates, Robert Colquhoun (b. 1914) and Robert MacBryde (b. 1914), began as Sutherland disciples too, but they have emerged as two of the most individual younger painters in England. Colquhoun in particular has found his way to an original style by crossing Wyndham Lewis' vorticism with those aspects of Sutherland's art which touch closely on Picasso's discoveries, using a faceted structure to fortify the plasticity of his figures and to provide a curious vibrating motion to his contours (opposite). His color is rich and luminous within a somber range of mustard yellows, greens and browns, and his iconography is occasionally charged with the *maudite* spirit which characterizes the art of the French painter, Balthus; his "realism," like Balthus', is brooding, acute, a little uneasy, intensely felt — and memorable. Widely traveled in Italy, France, Belgium and Holland, Colquhoun works with a vigor and conviction which made him appear, in the exhibition of contemporary British painting organized in 1946 by the Albright Art Gallery of Buffalo, as already the peer of his more experienced elders. Unfortunately, only one painting by MacBryde has arrived in this country, so far as I know, but many qualified English critics consider him as promising as Colquhoun, and his *Performing Clown* (page 150) is an impressive work for so young an artist.

Finally, there are a few painters in England today whose work parallels the trance-like imagery of "apocalyptic" poets like Dorian Cooke, Dylan Thomas, Henry Treece, Norman McCaig and others. Of these artists Cecil Collins seems the most gifted, and in his paintings and drawings Blake replaces Samuel Palmer as the motivating source of an art which depends on primitivism of wonder, absolute repudiation of mundane affairs, a reaffirmation of faith in ecstasy and revelation. Collins was born in Plymouth in 1908, was trained at the Plymouth School of Art and then, for four years, at the Royal College of Art. He began to exhibit in 1935, and was included in the London International Surrealist Exhibition of 1936. Since that date he has progressed to a more personal fantasy, though his debt to Blake, Picasso and André Masson is apparent, and he has sometimes arrived at eclectic mannerism when what he sought was visional white heat. Yet from the evidence of the color plates in a recent monograph on Collins, his art has an eerie charm, particularly in his series of "Fools." Moreover, it is an encouraging sign that his paintings, though their color is applied as tinting in the manner of the Gothic illumi-

Robert MacBryde: Performing Clown, 1946. *Oil. 36 x 28″. The Lefevre Gallery, London.*

nators, seem more confident than his drawings. And he has gone beyond — at least he has kept clear of — the romantic naturalism of Palmer-Sutherland-Piper — to reopen an esteemed vein in English art.

There are undoubtedly many other younger artists of talent in England today, many of them retarded in development by long service in the war. It is too early, of course, to say

Francis BACON: Study for "Man with Microphones," 1946. *Oil, 57 x 50½". The Lefevre Gallery, London.*

whether for them the revival of indigenous lyricism, so widespread now, will prove decisive. On many of them Paris may once again exert its old and powerful sway. It should be remembered in any case that even during the recent years of re-emphasis on native authority in art, Picasso has remained a spiritual Prince Consort in England, accompanied by a Continental court from which many of the British painters mentioned in these pages have learned vital lessons. Yet the contemporary English school is making its own serious statement. One wishes that it were heard more often and more fully in this country.

151

Due